Oui

Ricardo-Martín Marroquín

Dedication:

To my family with whom God continues to bless me with.
Thank you, dad for your loving sacrifice!

Acknowledgements:

It is always a great joy to thank so many people that have encouraged me to keep on writing and to share ideas, thoughts and feelings through *the art of the pen*. First of all, I am so thankful to our Lord for giving me an earthly father who sacrificed his career and his comfortable life for the well-being of our family. He endured much discouragement and danger, putting his life at risk, for the sake of my mom, my sister and me. I also am very grateful for my mom's love and direction, especially when she had to take on both parental roles. With the support of her brother, Luis and other family members, she painted a vision of hope and possibilities, both in Peru and in Canada. Her loving and caring touch was always present. To my wife who supports me by listening to my stories, those that make it on paper and those that are simply orally. Thank you for always smiling. To my kids who everyday are teaching me how to become a loving daddy, and never get tired of listening to anecdotes. To my uncle Luis, who became a father figure not just for my sister and me, but to the many cousins who needed a mentor. Finally, I have many friends and colleagues (at Redeemer University and at the HWDSB) and family members, some of which have been depicted in this story, who I want to express my sincere gratitude, especially to my friend Roberto, who took the time to read and provide me with purposeful feedback. To Fenny, Horacio, and to all of you who extended your arms and gave us a warm welcome. To all of you, thank you! This feat is ours.

To all the people who woke up with a new sunrise, and a limitless horizon.

Table of Content:

Chapter 1 – The Beginning of It All — pp. 7

Chapter 2 – The Goodbye: Martín Father's Journey Begins — pp. 15

Chapter 3 – Terrorism and The Struggles — pp. 24

Chapter 4 – Martín, The One Once Known As "The Champion" — pp. 35

Chapter 5 – For The Love of Baseball — pp. 47

Chapter 6 – The Phone Calls — pp. 56

Chapter 7 – The Wintery Month — pp. 68

Chapter 8 – The Next Phone Call — pp. 84

Chapter 9 – The New "Extended Family" in Canada — pp. 90

Chapter 10 – Baseball, The Other Beautiful Game — pp. 101

Chapter 11 – The Story of Mo — pp. 113

Chapter 12 – Martín's Best Friend in Peru — pp. 124

Chapter 13 – The Departure of Mo — pp. 135

Chapter 14 – Terror with a Sweet Victory — pp. 150

Chapter 15 – The Surprise — pp. 156

Chapter 1 – The Beginning of It All

The bell had rung, and all the pupils went outside for recess. They quickly scattered throughout the playground; some choosing the monkey bars, while others playing on the field. However, Martín did not know where to go or what to do. The first thing that crossed his mind was to sneak out to the outside wall where he had been standing since the beginning of recess. His reasoning for doing so was in hopes of joining a group of boys from his grade 5 class that had started to play "Red Wall"; a game where they threw a tennis ball with all their might against the wall where he was originally standing. Quickly he realized the idea of the game and thought it was fun. He did not know how to ask to play since he did not speak any English as he had just arrived to Canada a few days earlier. The game consisted of a player throwing the ball against the wall, and it would rebound off the wall forming a trajectory of a big loop that usually would go above everyone's head.

Martín extended his arm and caught the ball with three fingers. Everyone was astonished at the grab but no one said anything except for a kid called Mo, who just screamed "hey, pass the ball!". Martín did not understand the exclamation of the boy and stayed frozen with his arm extended, still holding the ball. Mo ran to Martín and forcefully took the ball out of his hands and then threw it against the wall. "You are out!" he shouted to Martín, who did not know the meaning of the words but understood that he was not allowed to play anymore. The game played on and the kids kept on running and tossing and screaming and laughing. All seemed to be having a great time. Martín could feel the joy of his peers and wanted to be part of this but again did not know how to get involved. In his mind, he could only think about how he wanted to play but not knowing his way into the activity, he just observed from the sideline. Another young boy who was a year older noticed that Martín could not speak English and called him to another wall. There he taught him the game by using single words and many actions that followed each command such as throw, run, duck, catch, out and win. Those two played the game for the next twenty minutes until the bell rang again, at which point everyone ran to form lines. Martín was not sure what was happening but he understood that he too had to get in line. That is exactly what he did. "Hey, my name is Richard" mentioned the boy who had just taught him how to play. Although this boy was not in the same class and therefore did not form part of the same line, he told Martín that he would play with him again. Martín did not understand a single word but could infer from the smile and the pat that he received on his back that Richard was the friend he needed and that he was a nice kid. That made him forget for a moment, the hardship he was enduring due to having left his extended family behind in his own country.

His smile quickly vanished with the strong wind of the reoccurring whiteouts, commonly felt in the middle of winter. Suddenly his mind took him back to the past, as it had done so many other times. It took him back to another line up... the one his parents and his sister were making outside the Embassy of the United States in Lima, Peru.

The morning was cold, damp and dark and Martín, Adriana and their parents Maya and Victor, had been standing in the line-up that felt like it lasted an eternity for a few hours without moving a single step. The Embassy did not open until nine in the morning but all of the candidates would form a line a few hours before, hoping to make it to the office and try their luck with an embassy representative. They planned to plead and beg as a second resort if their initial argument to why being allowed into the USA was denied. This was not the first nor second time standing in the lineup outside the U.S. embassy, and although the family did not want to get rejected once again, they thought that the third time was the charm. Martín's dad felt that the best thing to do for the family was to flee the country (for crucial reasons to be explained), and if this meant sacrificing a night's rest, then he would have his family endure this.

During that lineup, Martín's dad, Victor, continued preparing the family on possible questions that the ambassador might ask. In fact, the family had spoken already with an uncle who lived in the United States. who suggested possible answers to potential questions. The night before, Martín practiced how to answer questions with his mom, while his sister did the same thing with her dad. The family knew how important it was to get prepared in order to convince the embassy of their case. The rehearsal of questions went almost all night until his mom realized how late into the evening it was. At that point both parents decided to end their practice and called it quits until the next day which was just a few hours away, where they would be in front of the ambassador.

The night before the lineup Martín and his sister went to their room after brushing their teeth and saying goodnight to their parents. However, both of them were wired with information overload and felt that they needed to continue the immigration discourse. Both of them stayed up talking about possible answers, and how these responses would give them a chance to earn their ticket to North America. They even started talking about living there and how majestic the snow-covered trees and houses would look like in the middle of winter. They had seen the snow in movies, but had never felt the essence of a flake on their bare skin or on the tip of their tongue. They saw themselves creating a snowman, building a snowy trench and forts where they would each take a side and target each other. Imagining the snowman that could be created by throwing voluminous snow balls, their fantasy took them to a winter wonderland where the cold was not an issue, yet the snow would fall down perfectly on the ground covering everything like a white blanket seen in the Andean Cordillera. They sighed at the same time and stayed quiet for a while, until his sister who was older said "goodnight". Shortly after, both fell asleep, but it would only have been a short nap due to the closeness of the wakeup call which was just a couple of hours away.

One thing is to practice the answers to these questions with your loved ones, but the moment you are facing an agent who has the power over your destiny (in his country), you can kiss goodbye your chances of formulating any satisfactory and convincing answer. This is exactly what happened once it was their opportunity to meet the ambassador. He took a quick look at the family and summoned Martín's dad, asking for the passports. After reviewing the case, he marked the documents with a red coloured "denied" stamp. Immediately, the family's hope for an opportunity to migrate, vanished, turning their fantasy into a delusion. Martín's dad tried his best to advocate his case but this was a waste of time that did not solidify into anything meaningful. By the time his mom got up to support her husband, the ambassador left the clerk's office and went inside a solid metal door that was protected by a guard officer. The mother held the dad, wrapping her arms around his shoulders while Martín's sister did the same thing to him. Both set of couples, one after the other, looked to the door with eyes filled with hopelessness, and left the embassy.

All four family members walked to the car where it was parked a few blocks away. It was one of the quietest walks that Martín and his sister could remember. Although the ride back home was unpleasant and the parents' hardship was visible in their faces, the mom still asked the dad to stop at a nearby bakery to have some treats. "What's there to celebrate?" dad asked. "The fact that we are still together" mom replied quickly with a soft smile.

"Hey are you coming in…" one of the kids from his class exclaimed with a negative and condescending tone. Even though Martín did not understand the sentence, he quickly inferred that the kid was not going to hold the door forever for him who remained lost in thought in a lineup that was once there. Quickly he moved and made it to the door before this one closed shut in front of him. He took in the warmth of the heat and felt once again safe and sound. Closing his eyes and taking a deep breath he thought of how blessed he was for making it to North America. Although his happiness for being in Canada had escalated to the highest degree, he still remembered the ones left behind, especially his uncles and cousins. His mind however, always travelled back home and there were several quiet moments while in school; moments that made others think that Martín could have some type of emotional or academic issue inferred by many because the lack of language. This time, he decided to smile and not think too much but rather to enjoy the moment.

Once inside and while taking off his winter coat, he noticed that his classmates went to the change room, so he followed the boys, not knowing what to do but to sit on a bench and wait for what was next. Suddenly everyone left the area and entered a big well-lit gym. There was a volleyball net in the middle, separating the playing area in even halves that also had lines on the ground that perfectly depicted the perimeter of a volleyball court. Two kids approached the teacher and suddenly started helping him take down the nets and posts. Martín was not too happy about this, as he thought that he would be playing volleyball. This was one sport that he enjoyed so much and the one where he and his sister created fond memories; ones that would be imprinted in his heart for the rest of his life. His mind quickly took him back to his old street back at home where he was enjoying a game of night volleyball in the company of the neighborhood kids. He and his sister enjoyed playing the sport with the friends where often as many as twenty kids would congregate in the dead-end street. One of the homeowners who had been a volleyball coach would use two light posts that happened to be located on opposite sides of the same road. It was these posts that he would tie the net to. The sidewalk would act as the area for the families to gather and watch the kids play. Sometimes Martín's family would come and watch the kids play the game with some of the other parents. They were all taught how to volley, hit, pass, and even how to play as a team. The joyous nights would continue with a championship game where bragging rights were earned and the loser team would just take down the net. Sometimes those final games could not get played, as the whole country was on a curfew that pretty much started an hour or two after it got dark. This was due to the terrorism that hurt and reigned the society. Nevertheless, numerous nights were filled with excitement and a few good games of competitive volleyball.

    A sudden noise, snapped Martín back in to reality of the present day. Everyone sat down on the floor with their back against the wall waiting for their name to be called by this new teacher. All of the students said "here" as their names were called, however, as Martín's name came up, there was silence. The teacher called it again, hoping to hear from the new boy, however, his pronunciation of the name was very much different to the one that Martín was accustomed to hearing. - Hey kid, are you Martin-, asked the teacher. Martín just looked up from his spot and with his big dark brown eyes, showed a degree of intimidation. Without saying a word, he turned his attention to a girl who manifested -yes he is but he can't speak-. -Oh… well just do what the others do-, mentioned the teacher and walked away back to the middle of the gym from where he was taking attendance. Once the teacher was finished, he gave instructions about a game the class was going to participate in and reminded everyone of the rules. Shortly after, he divided the class into two equal teams of boys and girls. The "ones" were on the left side, whereas the "twos" were on the right side. Martín was nominated as a "one" but ended up not understanding the whereabouts of his number, so ended up walking towards the wrong side. No one said anything to him and he did not mention a word, not only because he could not say anything in English, but because he did not feel comfortable to participate or express anything.

The whistle went and the kids ran to the middle line that separated them and quickly tried grabbing a ball before someone from the other team did. Once they did so, they whipped the ball against a player on the other team. Some were hit in a different part of the body, while others caught the ball in the air. Martín evaded the ball, as it was coming towards him as a projectile. He quickly realized that this was what he needed to do, that is to say, move out of the way to avoid getting hurt. What he did not realize however, was that he could also grab a ball and do the same as the other kids, and throw it with all his might. The game was coming to an end and there were three kids left, Martín on one side and two other kids on the other. One of those was Mo, who grabbed a ball ran to the line and threw a perfect ball that landed precisely on Martín's chest. It ricocheted off the body up into the air, about two meters, and then Martín grabbed it. This meant that Mo had to sit on the ground where the rest of his team was already, chanting his name and making loud noises showing their expressions quite obvious. Mo was upset at the fact that he was out, and therefore, quickly grabbing another ball and without the teacher noticing he pitched it against Martín, hitting him on the nape. This impeded the fallen soldier to notice the throw that the last kid on Mo's team had also done a second later which landed on the leg of Martín. All the kids on that team jumped with joy and celebrated their win with Mo. Whereas, Martín felt embarrassed, impotent and very much confused as he did not understand the dissatisfaction of his own team towards him. No one from the team dared said anything against Mo or what he did. Everyone just took the loss and tried turning the page.

The game continued on and it seemed like Martín was getting the hang of it. However, every time he felt like celebrating an accomplishment such as grasping the idea of the game or becoming better at it, Mo would blow off Martín's happiness by getting him out each and every time. It seemed like Mo and his friends understood that the new kid, the immigrant, was good and therefore, it was necessary to get him out as soon as possible. Unfortunately for Martín, he did not understand the level of competition and could not understand why Mo was so harsh with him. This lead him to daydream, and think about his past terribly missing his hometown. The procession he kept inside and although he tried his best to please his parents (by trying his best), the lack of language naturally made him quiet, disengaged and at times, even bored.

Chapter 2 – The Goodbye: Martín Father's Journey Begins

It is fairly common to miss those left behind when one is an immigrant. It is also very common for your mind to travel back to the past, especially when struggle strikes you down. For Martín, this was his first few months after arriving in Canada, the "Majestic". His mind played tricks on him, sometimes forcing him to revisit scenarios that were painful and brought him no joy, and even though he did not control these thoughts, they kept on crawling back to his present, forcing him to travail more so in a new country, especially when learning the language and ways of life. One of these occasions that Martín remembered was one that he would have wanted to erase from his repertoire. That is, the day his dad left Peru in search for the so-called "American Dream".

It was customary to have the extended family, relatives and friends visit every time one would leave the country, and this is precisely what happened to Martín. Many family members and friends came over, immediately after dinner the day before, and beside saying goodbye to their cherished Victor, also known as "el Negrito[1]", some of them helped with weighing bags, picking up a few last-minute items, dropping off farewell gifts and even bringing bags of groceries for the rest of the family that was staying behind. In this case, it was only Martín's dad

---

[1] It is important to clarify that in Latin America the word *Negrito*, though depicting a person by the colour black, is neither racist nor inappropriate. In fact, parents would use this "nickname" to differentiate between their kids that sometimes in a Hispanic home would have very diversed (in skin colour) kids.

who was leaving the country while the rest of the family (the mom and sister, along with Martín) stayed back. The fact that more than twenty people came over that evening, made it easier for Martín not to dwell in pain and sorrow from having his father about to leave the country. In fact, it was very much needed. His cousins and uncles that visited made his mind distracted with planning different events in the near future that would help ease the pain of not having his dad around. There was even a point in time that evening where he actually forgot that his dad was leaving the next day. However, every occasion he would pass by the living room where all of the luggage was laid down, spreading all over the living room floor, it reminded him that for an indefinite period he would be fatherless.

His cousin invited Martín to a kids' television show where they would have the opportunity to appear on the show. This made him look forward to something in the future. His cousin had thought it all out, such as the transportation to and fro, the food, the permission from Martín's parents, and even getting his room ready for the slumber party after the show. They were both very close in age and more so in heart, therefore it was good that they had each other, especially during difficult moments. Cousins have that calming way of being. They sooth the soul in ways that others cannot, and for Martín this was exactly what anyone would have advised; playdates with his cousin.

Martín however still felt sad for his family as it was the first time that they would be torn apart by an unknown amount of time and by so many kilometers. In fact, his family had always made sure to spend their time together. They would eat together and take vacation trips often. His dad however, felt that this sacrifice was necessary for the family's well-being and future.

Uncles and family stepped up to the plate to help out with the numerous needs that the family would encounter. A couple of family members in particular, adopted Martín's family for time they remained in Peru. Uncle Luchín would make sure that both Martín and his sister, Adriana would be busy with homework, literature, and extra-curricular activities. The uncle would teach both kids about different authors, and modern plays. He would teach them how to become critical thinkers in today's society. In fact, he would take them to plays occasionally and after the show, they would go to a Chinese restaurant, to eat and discuss the performance. He instilled culture in their minds and it was for this reason that Martín would be volunteered by his teacher to recite poems during special assemblies. Martín would be a third grader who would have been the student to recite by memory César Vallejo's Los Heraldos Negros or Nicomedes Santa Cruz' La pelona[2]. A younger version of Martín would stand in front of his peers, five hundred of them, and they would all attentively listen as he started his discourse. The interesting part was that his homeroom teacher, Señorita María, watching from the side where all of the faculty sat together, would join him in his performance, repeating all of the lyrics without making any sound. It was very clear that she enjoyed his recitations. For his uncle, this was a feat. He always wanted the kids to strive in all they did, although his main goal was for them to be remembered as kind hearted and active contributors to society. Even though he had his own house where he lived, he would spend the main part of his day with Martín's family, not trying to replace a father figure but rather becoming one.

---

[2] Both César Vallejo and Nicomedes Santa Cruz were Peruvian writers, whose literary work made an important contribution to the country's culture.

Martín's sister, Adriana, enjoyed theatre and public speaking. His uncle noticed these two attributes of hers and decided to place her in drama club. There she learned many skills that would become very favourable in her career. She enjoyed her lessons but sometimes it seemed like Martín would enjoy them even more, as he would sit behind the stage and mimic her actions. Then he would use these for the next time he was invited to recite a new poem.

Uncle Luchín was not the only member that would come and help Martín's family. In fact, another family member that would come on a weekly basis to make sure that there were no needs with both the kids and Maya, was Victor's younger brother, and his name was José. The interesting fact about him was that he would ask the kids' mom for permission to come pick up Martín and his sister. He would bring them to his house where the two became like his own children along with the other three children he already had, who were anxiously waiting for their cousins to enjoy their time together. Although the kids loved spending time with the cousins, the permission was sometimes rejected due to some prior engagement. However, when they were allowed to visit the family, they had a memorable time. One of those was climbing all the way up to a small mountain that for the kids seemed the size the Machu Picchu[3]. Sometimes they would only make it to the middle of the mountain but in one occasion they achieved their goal. Wow, what a view of the city they had in front of them! Anywhere they turned, they could see a spectacular panoramic outlook of their city. Although the night time was the best to watch all of the city lights, it became more

---

[3] Machu Picchu is one of the Seven Wonders of the World. Located in the Sierra of Peru, this ruin was known for its imminent and important presence for the Incan empire.

difficult to climb up (or down), and for this reason their adventurous trekking would only take place during the day.

These were just a few of the memories evoked that would help ease the pain of not having a father around anymore. Standing in front of the luggage with his dad and family members helping out with the items, Martín's sorrow reminded him of the reality on which he was about to embark. He tried keeping it together, more so to show his parents that he was mature and to show his dad that in his absence he would be able to imitate him and take care of the women in the home, nevertheless, this was all just a task too troublesome for a ten-year-old. The flight down the stairs from the third floor was always a fast one, and Martín had races with dad going up and down, sometimes winning, sometimes losing. This time it seemed like both father and son wanted the descending to take as long as possible; they wanted to cherish each step down, hoping that it would not be their last one, but maybe the only one for a while. It is difficult to hold back tears when they want to burst out of you for a good reason, it is even more challenging to hold them in when going down the stairs with a loved one that is about to depart. Once downstairs, there were three cars, two of them were family member's vehicles and the other one was a taxi. All three cars got filled with family members. In one of them Mom, dad, son and daughter came in whereas in the other ones, there were all of the family members that had come to say goodbye.

The trip to the airport was filled with silence in the back seat. Although mom tried making conversation with the kids, they both decided to look out their windows and busy their minds with the habitual Lima traffic. On the other hand, the dad talked to the driver and had conferred his plan to make it to the United States. The driver agreed with the dad and told him to take good care of himself, as he knew firsthand how long that journey would be. - Don't trust anyone and don't think of anyone as your friend. Everyone wants to fulfill their personal interest and whomever you think of a friend will leave you behind when times get tough -, the driver suggested to Victor. This was a wakeup call for Martín's dad as he was not entirely sure what he would encounter in his voyage.

Suddenly, the taxi made it to the airport and in what seemed like a split second all of the bags and people were out of the vehicle. They all made their way through a crowd to the appropriate line where the dad would pick up his airplane ticket and drop off his two bags. While he was doing this, the rest of the family stayed together in an area of the airport and they talked and laughed and tried to make the best out of tough times. Then dad came back to where the family, extended family, relatives and friends were congregating, and mentioned that it was time for him to start making his way to the gate, at which point he had to say goodbye to everyone. First, the friends hugged him and wished him well, reminding him to be careful and to commend his ways in the Lord's hands. Then the cousins and nephews did the same thing, kissing him on the cheek and reminding him that his family would be in good hands. Finally, Victor approached the immediate family… His wife although tried to be strong for the kids and her husband's sake at that moment she felt his hug, almost fainted and started sobbing. Martín and Adriana were the last ones to say goodbye to their dad and both were already sobbing the moment he made eye contact with them both. Adriana grabbed onto her dad and would not let go, whereas Martín started showing a feeling of anger towards him for leaving him. This made him not want to say goodbye. It took his mom to talk to him and explain to him that dad was doing this for their future. Demands such as – why does he have to leave? Why can't we all go together? –, escaped his mouth. – Son, I will only be separated from you for a bit so that one day we can all be together always –, he quickly interjected. These were the right words for Martín to end his grudge and quickly join his sister in hugging his dad. – I will miss you so much–, he uttered. – I will miss you in every single breath –, dad replied. All four hugged for what seemed like a split second while the relatives and friends were moved to tears. – Brother, it is time –, said Martín's uncle, grabbing the carry-on and placing the belt around the traveler's shoulder. Martín's dad accepted the bag, gave his wife and kids one last kiss, and then turned to the relatives and friends and thanked them all for their willingness to help his family during his absence. His walk towards the gate was accompanied by everyone's eyes, especially Adriana and Martín who stuck their noses on the glass and would not move from their spot, as they saw daddy vanish in the distance of the long hallway. The pain that ran down their cheeks started a burning sensation that made their faces turn red. They felt hopeless and helpless and could not fathom having their family as only three members. This struck them in the most profound part of their soul.

Deep in thought, Victor pondered whether he had made the right decision. That is, to leave behind his family to seek a better place to live. He waited at the gate until he was called to board. Until that time, he had kept his cool and had not shown any sensitive emotions, however, the moment that he took his seat and put on his seatbelt, everything seemed to have sunken down to his core. Immediately his eyes swelled up, forcing him to tuck his own head between his arms as he started crying like a baby. He could only think of his beloved family and hoped to God that his sacrifice of leaving them behind would bear some kind of fruit, that for now he could not imagine. His pain was so noticeable that the flight attendant understood not to bother him with anything but rather to bring him a drink, some food and a few napkins. Victor raised his head and took the offer from the lady's hand. She understood his pain and during the flight she made sure to pass by and make sure that Victor had everything that he needed to make his voyage more enjoyable. Thank God, that no one sat beside him, for this meant that Victor had a whole row to stretch his legs. He just kept on thinking about his wife and kids and had to remind himself about his plans for a better future. Up from the sky and looking out the window, he gazed at the clouds and kept on thinking about this plan.

– Martin –, the teacher called out. – Martin –, repeating in a stronger and louder voice since the newcomer did not reply. – I don't think he can talk –, mentioned one of the students, and the other kids laughed with the exception of one girl whose name was Rose. She was born in China and was fairly new to Canada but knew enough English to communicate and to understand everything that both the teacher and the students said to her. The fact that she went to an English school in her home country also helped. Moreover, her parents hired her a couple of tutors to help her with literacy and with numeracy. She was very advanced with English for her brief time immersed in the culture. She understood perfectly well how Martín felt and so she would just sit beside him and hand him his work. Sometimes she would even explain things to him, slowly and with a smile, which made Martín feel safer. It took a young kid to help him realize that learning was possible. Martín could feel that this young girl had good intentions and wanted to help him. Sometimes it seemed like she would protect him from some of the bullies in the class. Although this was a good thing for Martín, sometimes he felt more embarrassed, as did not like having a girl defend him from his issues. – The kid can't even defend himself –, was one of the things that Mo would taunt him with, which still made things worse for Martín. One time however, he was very happy that Rose jumped in to help him out, and that was when Mo with two other followers decided to push him around in the hallway. Rose had gone to the bathroom and on her way back to class, she saw the boys doing exactly that, bullying the new kid, and after a few times of pleading to them to leave her friend alone, she decided to lift her leg and kick as high as Mo's forehead without touching him but letting him know what she was capable of if they did not stop. The boys decided to run off to the classroom and without mentioning not even one word of what had just happened, they sat down quietly in their own chairs and continued their work. Even the teacher noticed that those boys were so well behaved and quiet all day thinking "what a change!" He did not even question it, even though at the beginning he was compelled to do so. Then he decided that it would be better to just leave it as that. Unfortunately for Martín, Rose only stayed in the school for only two more weeks, as her parents had decided to accept a medical position in another part of town, which forced them to move, and for Rose to go to a new school. On her last day, Rose approached the boys and excused herself for the incident they had with her a couple of weeks before, but then reminded them that if they bugged Martín again, that she would come back to hunt them down. – No, no, it is fine. Martín is our friend…–, declared Mo right away with a nervous face hoping that the last incident would not repeat again, especially in front of the whole class. And this is exactly what happened. Mo learned very quickly that he could not bother Martín anymore. However, as much as we would love to say that things seemed better for him, unfortunately, this was not the case, and any small issue brought him back to his native country.

Chapter 3 – Terrorism and The Struggles –

– We cannot stay here any longer–, confirmed Victor to Maya, his wife.

– Yes, but how are we going to get to the United States if we get denied entry every time? It's impossible to do so! – she replied.

– If I don't leave I don't know what we will do if something happens to one of us (Victor was referring to the assassination of his uncle who had the same name as he did, in addition to the two occasions where he suffered two bomb attacks while at work in the bank. Victor worked as an auditor across the country, performing financial audits for the government and for private corporations. Certain people in power wanted him to cover up for what is known as financial fraud. Victor however, would not accept any bribery, even if this would enrich his family.) I cannot have the kids live in fear that something could happen to one of us. And what if something happens to… –

– Never mention that!" –, Maya cut him off without letting him finish his last sentence.

What had happened was that the day the family got the third and last rejection of the American embassy, Victor received a visitor (sent by a cousin from the US) to talk to him about another way to get to the USA. The plan was vaguely disclosed but the end goal was the highlight, to make it to the final destination. That night, Maya took the kids to visit their cousins while Victor stayed home and spent a good hour talking about this new plan with the visitor. The strategy was simple: the agency that this man represented would take him to Mexico on a one-way airfare, with one stop in Panama City, Panama. The idea was that after landing in Mexico City, he would travel to Los Angeles with all the documents in place. Although Victor had so many queries, the man only guaranteed the outcome but reiterated that he could not disclose too much information about the plan, otherwise people would abuse the system, and then the whole scheme would go down. Although the man only gave Victor a very short time to think it through, he pondered on this trip so much that his head seemed like it was going to explode. He did not know how to explain it to his wife, and this was in part for the lack of information. This also meant that he would have to deposit a couple of thousands of American dollars to pay for all of the travel expenses, but due to the previous expense of the US embassy, the money was not readily available.

That same night, once his wife and kids got home, Victor helped the kids with their nightly routine and put them to bed. Maya noticed him a bit anxious and could feel that he wanted to talk to her. She boiled a pot of water to make some chamomile for their anticipated chat, hoping that this would calm her beloved. Once the kids were in their bedroom and falling asleep, Victor explained the happenings with the visitor and what he thought of doing.

– This is a great opportunity for us to make it to the United States –, he mentioned.

– But what about us? What would we do without you? What will I do with two kids by myself? – were a few of the questions that stormed Maya's head.

– It will only be temporarily, as once I make it, I will send for you three – promised Victor to an already anguished wife. As his spouse, she already knew that whatever came in his head would be difficult for him to get out. She suddenly felt the anticipated loneliness that would accompany her sooner than she expected it.

– Please, do not say anything to the children. I don't want them to worry about you leaving just yet –, begged the mom.

Unfortunately for her, Adriana was behind the door and heard nearly the entire dialogue, and wanting to tell her little brother, she abruptly woke him up. To his dismay, he could not fall asleep after this and kept her up for close to the whole night.

The next morning, Victor felt much better about his new plan and that this might be the right choice. Maya had learned to trust in him even when she felt like going against his will. This time it was very tough to do so, however, she did not disappoint him. She was saddened to just think that her family would be divided due to time and distance. This was something new to her but trusted her gut on this. The next day she accompanied Victor to the agency to pay the deposit in order to secure his spot. There he found out the details of the plan, such as when he would embark the plane, how long he would need to stay in Mexico and how he would arrive to the "Land of the Free".

At the agency, the majority of people were men, however there were a couple of women willing to try their luck. Everyone was promised comfortable accommodations, three meals a day and time for sightseeing in specific locations with a professional tour guide. The cost seemed reasonable and the gains were huge. There was now no doubt in anyone's mind. The only catch was that the full payment needed to be done within one week and there needed to be a deposit by the next day. Many people signed up for this deal and tried selling some of their possessions like their cars, appliances and even their apartments so that they would have enough money to pay the fees, and also some extra to take on their new endeavor. Some even asked their family members to continue selling their possessions and to wire their money to the United States once they arrive there. People were overjoyed to this news. This was the "once in a lifetime opportunity" and an answer of hope that Martín's dad was awaiting.

Victor and Maya both went to the meeting and heard the same story from the tour guide. However, each came out with a different conclusion, which led to one being happy and the other full of sadness. – This is an answer to prayer –, Victor mentioned, while, Maya felt discomforted and very anxious. She did not trust the system and felt that there was a catch. Maybe her sixth sense as a woman allowed her to feel something that Victor did not perceive. By the time the deadline came to pay out the balance, Victor only had a big portion of it, so he decided to go to the agency and ask if it was possible to let his wife pay the remainder of the fee once she was able to sell a few more items. The agency agreed to this as long as he was willing to pay by a stipulated later date which also included a nominal fee. – No problem, it shall be done –, affirmed Victor.

The time came when the secret of the trip was to be shared with both Adriana and Martín. Although this happened by the kitchen table in their own house, Victor would have preferred to have the conversation at an ice-cream parlour, to help mask their sadness with a treat. Adriana, being the oldest asked several questions that she had formulated ever since the moment that she snuck behind the door and heard part of the conversation that night when Victor informed Maya. The main one that both parents could not answer was "is it worth it for us to be apart?" Victor knew the answer but also knew that nothing in their life was worth separating the family, so he stayed quiet, hoping that Maya would majestically answer. As for Martín, he stayed very quiet and only stared out into space. His silence revealed his emotions. However, it went unnoticed, and perhaps because his sister communicated her discomfort with so many words, the parents overlooked the son's feelings. Martín did not worry though, as he had his older sister to enquire enough for him, and felt a bit comforted that everything would go well. In his ten years of age, he had managed to believe that his dad was a superhero and that he was the smartest person on the planet. Therefore, he did not feel the it necessary to worry, although he was still not pleased with having his dad leave home.

That night Maya went to bed by herself, since Victor decided to stay in the living room, meditating on what he had just committed to. He kept on beating himself up with the "did I do the right thing". However, he knew that living in a very unstable situation due to terrorism and economic turmoil was not the paradise he constantly promised his family. What turned the scale were three separate incidents that his family had suffered, Victor specifically. Although, nothing was done on his behalf, this time he did not want to stay cross armed.

The first event happened a few years ago, when both Martín and Adriana were a baby and a toddler respectively. Victor was a chartered accountant and worked in various banks doing audits for the government. His job was to unmask briberies, illegal handling of money and of course corruption of all sorts. During that time, a terrorist group was gaining power in many regions of the country, especially outside of the capital, and this group would gain more power by going to the citizens and asking for their support. Failure to help out or oppose "the cause" was deemed a penalty, and most of the times paid with blood. This time when he was on a work trip, Victor was asked by a well-known and shady investor to allow him to borrow a significant amount of money from the bank for an investment that had no collateral. Since Victor had access to the funds, although he was not a banker, he would usually be asked for these types of favours. He however, had learned very early in his career to walk a straight line without straying neither to the left nor to the right, a teaching that his own father had always mentioned, especially when he found out that Victor wanted to get into this career. "Son, you are either a good accountant who does the right thing, or you are one who gets his hands dirty for others, and with those hands you feed your own family. It is up to you to decide." Victor knew what his father's teaching was, and he wanted to follow the same footsteps imprinted in the same path that his dad had already taken. Unfortunately, due to not getting involved in the business of "the cause", the terrorist group set up a bomb in the bank that detonated precisely as Victor had just finished working there. He had literally just closed the bank with a colleague and had taken a few steps from the branch. This meant that the only thing that he suffered was a scar on his right leg produced by a shattered glass window that penetrated his work pants. Due to the explosion and the end product, both he and his colleague were taken to the emergency room for further examinations, but then released once they were deemed fine. The news travelled home to his wife faster than he could imagine. By the time, he decided to call home, that is, when he arrived at the hotel from the hospital, his wife had already called the concierge and had left a few messages, frantically needing to know how he was doing. It took a lot of love to calm her down and to comfort her via a long-distance call. That night both Victor and Maya, stayed up a few hours talking on the phone until she was too tired to hold the phone to her ear. However, not wanting to let go of him, he hung up after singing her a love song, just like when they were dating.

The second scenario had a different outcome, as this one did harm Victor. This incident also happened away from home. Another investor who was associated with the same terrorist group mentioned earlier, came to see Victor. He too asked for the same investment support that his colleague had once asked. This rang a bell for Victor, as he recognized the plan from the investor and wanted to say no, but feared for his life. Victor, excused himself to go to the kitchen and get his client and himself a cup of coffee. However, while his client was waiting in the office for his hot cup of java and did not realize anything weird, Victor was in the kitchen making a call to the police station. Sooner than Victor had anticipated, the police officers came in through the back door and trapped the man, handcuffed him and took him to the station for further questioning. Victor felt at peace and knew that he had done the right thing. Unfortunately, that man that was taken by the police was seen in that same act (handcuffed and escorted to the cruiser) by one of comrades and immediately reported the incident to their leader, who then commanded to place a "gift" by the main door of the branch. So, the moment that Victor was about to leave that same day after a full day of work, a bomb exploded, throwing him and a couple of other employees off their chairs. As for Victor, the force of the bomb threw him out of the window and ended up landing outside by the cars parked in the parking lot. The ambulance responded very promptly and took the three wounded to the nearby hospital. Out of the three employees affected, Victor was the one whose suffering was the greatest. He was in a coma and remained in the hospital for several weeks. Maya who ended up finding out the news on TV, immediately flew to his rescue, leaving both kids with her younger siblings to be taken care of. His recovery was very slow and even considered a difficult road by the doctors, but the moment the wife arrived (just a day after the incident) it was a miracle... Victor opened his eyes, became aware, started talking and even tried yanking his IV out of his forearm in a form of panic, and wanted to get out of his bed. It took three doctors and two male nurses to calm him down, although one could attribute his change in behavior to the soothing voice of his own wife that made him serene so that the other five professionals could connect him to the machine once again. At the beginning, he did not understand why he was prostrated on a hospital bed, and it took Maya to remind him not necessarily of the accident suffered, but of the help he would need for a few more days. Initially Victor kept asking what had happened to him but little by little and fairly fast, he started recuperating his memory and realized that he had suffered a terrorist attack while being at work. The unfortunate part was that Victor recuperated his memory late at night while all of the patients and spouses were already asleep. That night, Victor woke up from his nightmare, screaming and even crying, completely in shock, realizing what had just happened to him. Once again, it took the touch of his wife and her soothing voice to calm him down and give him comfort. That night he cried like a little baby while in the arms of his beloved, and once he succeeded to falling asleep, Maya snuggled right beside him. The bed although very small, was the perfect size for Victor to feel safe. When the doctor came with an injection to help calm Victor, Maya instantly rejected the medicine and forbade the doctor from administering it to her husband. – He is now calm. Please leave him alone –, she mentioned as she kept on stroking Victor's forehead.

Victor did not last too long in the hospital, as he healed very quickly. His work allowed him to travel back home and told him to take time to recuperate at home with the attention of his family. On the other hand, Victor felt the urge to go back to work once he had attained most of his energy. Although he felt stronger on the inside, he was weak and vulnerable on the inside. However, not knowing what he could do, he tried forgetting this event. For the kids, it was thrilling to have their daddy at home and play with them. If you were to ask Martín about this event now, he probably would not remember it, as he was just a baby.

The third incident was the one that really scared Victor. A few months before starting his plans to travel to the USA, he received a call from one of his aunts, Camila, who had just lost her husband. Victor the IV was the name of Victor's (Martín's dad) uncle. He had just been murdered by the same terrorist group who had come to his farm asking for monetary support. The idea was simple, to either support "the cause" with whatever they asked for, or to basically suffer the consequence. His uncle did not believe in violence, in the communist ideology that "the cause" had or even in the methods used to achieve their goals. For these reasons, he decided not to lend a hand neither by giving money, land or resources. He was warned and then reminded that they knew about his family affairs and their whereabouts, hoping that with this information he would change his mind. Once again, the uncle stated that he would not be seen making deals with terrorists. His reply was short and to the point, but so was their answer to him, as they did not miss a single shot, having landed just about everywhere in his body right outside his home. His fall was speedy and some would say that he did not have time to agonize. This fact, at least consoled the wife just a bit. Many neighbours came to take care of the body and support the new widow. Bleach was used for cleaning the floor, as the many tears the wife and kids shed by the door where he laid still, did not wash away the blood stains that tainted the footsteps of the house.

Victor loved his uncle and could not believe that he was now gone. For him this was surreal, as just a few days before the dark event, he had spoken with him and had even made plans to see him soon. He remembered his childhood days with his uncle. Victor's dad used to take him and his brothers to the uncle's ice-cream shop where all of the kids would enjoy a sweet and cool treat, just what the doctor ordered for hot sunny days. His uncle showed his love to all of his nephews and was even considered a father figure to them. He also enjoyed having his older brother come visit with the kids. He would always share a sweet creamy snack with all of the kids, and even before his brother and nephews would leave to go back home, the uncle would make sure to send them with a case of fresh produce, a few kilos of meats and poultry and even a sack of grains and oats. The uncle already knew that his brother (Victor's dad) would decline the goods, and for this reason, he would pack the trunk of the vehicle with the help of the nephews, and at the end, he would give them all an allowance. His soft temperament, loving character and willingness to share with everyone, made him not only special to his family but rather to the entire community. His own kids thought of him as a loving figure that ended up leaving this earth far too soon.

Tears rolled down Victor's cheek damping the cuff of his work shirt. This event made it clearer for him that he was making the right decision, that is to say, to leave his native land in search for a new country. His biggest nightmare was what would happen to his family if the same group decided to target him again through his own family. He could live if he was targeted but not if his family was harmed. He quickly got up from the couch and put down his newspaper took a deep breath and felt secure that he was doing the right thing, although in the back of his mind he was hoping and praying that he was making the right choice.

Maya saw her husband on the couch and after sitting with him for just a couple of minutes, she decided to leave him be to meditate and ask God for guidance. Once Victor left the living room, he visited his two kids in their room where they were both already laying down slumbering until the next day's morning. He kissed their foreheads and quietly uttered "I love you so much. May the good Lord protect you and keep you safe". He then went to meet his wife in their bedroom. Maya, although she felt that she needed to be more critical of the new endeavor, stayed quiet, knowing that questioning it would only bring dissatisfaction to her husband. So quietly she laid in bed with her eyes closed. However, the moment she felt the arm of her husband on her body, she quickly turned to face him and cuddled by his chest.

The day of the departure came faster than expected, and as mentioned before, the extended family helped Martín and his family feel better. Now on the plane, Victor could only think of his family and kept reminding him that sooner than later they would all be together, and that their sacrifice would be rewarded with lifelong happiness in North America.

Chapter 4 – Martín, The One once known as "the champion"

Martín's sister Adriana woke him up to go to school but he did not want to get up. Ever since he started attending his new Canadian school, he started losing interest in going to class. His parents could not understand the reason why, they just thought that he was battling with depression. His sister on the other hand, was enjoying her school, and had made friends with kids from all parts of the world. Both Maya and Victor thought that it was time for Martín to make friends too, but did not know why he would not. The lack of language also impeded the parents to approach the teacher and ask for his support. His dad just thought that this was only a stage, and that sooner or later, he would snap out of it, while his mom hoped that it would be sooner rather than later.

As for Mo, he went back to his old self and it seemed like he became nastier to Martín, as if he had to compensate for all of the missed time – You are useless –, he mentioned in a strong voice to Martín, when he dropped the ball while playing flag football. Mo showed his discontentment towards Martín because his team ended up losing a point and subsequently the game. Fortunately for Martín, he did not know what Mo had exclaimed, however, was able to read the body language and expression in his face, which at the end scared him and made him very uncomfortable. He ended up feeling useless and a nobody, which for him were new feelings. He did not know how to deal with them, so he would either try faking a sickness to miss out on school or think of his past.

The day was December 23, 1988 and the tournament was the Peruvian National Championship of Karate. Martín represented his district in the U10 competition. Although he was one of the youngest in his group, he seemed to be the one with the greatest potential in the sport. His coaches were thrilled with his accomplishment in such a short period of time, and felt like Martín was at the launch of his career. The support that he had from his dad and his uncle allowed him to feel secure, strong and a winner. He also practiced day and night every single day. This sport gave him conviction, a sense of pride yet humility, and confidence. Especially after he struggled greatly to read from early on in his life. In fact, that same year that he started the sport, he learned how to read. That tournament was a full day and the one to rise to the top in his category was precisely, Martín. He defeated kids his age and a year older. He was practically on cloud nine and his family did not want to burst that bubble. His accomplishment was shared with everyone in the family. Even his sister felt a sense of satisfaction, as she too helped him train. In fact, it seemed like everyone in his immediate family, including his uncle Luchín, helped Martín get prepared. It truly took a village to raise him to become successful in this mystical sport. He truly felt like a champion.

His first rival was a kid that was a year older than he was and who happened to have at least one foot in height on him. This lad was also representing a very prestigious dojo[4] in his city and had the support not only of his peers, but also of his own family, who had travelled a few hours to watch him become the next champion. Before Martín faced him, his uncle reminded him that it did not matter how tall a tree was, as its weakness was found at the bottom where an arborist with a few

---

[4] A martial arts studio.

swings of the axe could chop him down. Martín understood the figure of speech and knew what to do for his first match. The kid on the other hand was aggressive and fast. However, Martín applied the sweeping technique and brought him down, not once but twice, allowing him to land the two points necessary to win the match. His opponent got up and showed his lack of sportsmanship by approaching Martín in an aggressive way, however, Martín did not let his guard down and made a crescent kick that ended up making impact on the face of the kid. Martín did not get disqualified due to the circumstances, but this allowed the fans and other teams to talk about him, and to remind their own participants to watch out.

The second contender Martín needed to face was a boy his age who happened to also be about the same size of him. Both seemed to be eager to advance to the next round but Martín's uncle reminded him to not think of the future now but rather to focus on what is in front of him. His sister had seen this boy fight his first match (the uncle sent her to investigate the battle going on to the side of them, and then to report any findings of the winner). She mentioned that he used his punches a lot, and that he went for head shots. His uncle then asked Martín what would be the best way to fight someone like that, and Martín replied – by using your legs for kicking –. – Good–, he said – and now go out there and show it –. Adriana was right. The boy kept on punching in all directions around Martín with no precision so much that it seemed like there were flies around his opponent. Martín, on the other hand kept on evading the shots and did not attack until he saw an opening which lasted a split second; enough time to land a kick on his chest and score his first point. The second point came faster than the first one, given that the boy came to Martín again, throwing punches in the first two seconds. This time Martín saw the opening and delivered another kick that landed on the side, scoring his second and definitive point to win the fight. There was an hour waiting period which allowed the facilitators to set up the stage. This also allowed the competitors to eat something light, stretch, and chat with their families and friends. Martín's dad and uncle took both Adriana and the combatant for a quick bite to eat before continuing the training. Adriana was the toughest one out of the three who helped him train, as she kept on reminding him that he had not won anything so far, and that he needed to focus even more, if he wanted to be victorious. While his dad massaged him on his back, his uncle kept on working with his breathing, making sure that he had this under control. The third and fourth matches were very similar to the second, and having won both of them, he made it to the final match.

The fight could not start any sooner for all four but once it did, Martín's dad, along with his uncle and sister stayed in Martín's corner until both gladiators had to step foot on the floor mats. Once both of them were ready to battle, they bowed to the referee and then to each other. Then they took their stance until the signal was given. None of the boys started an attack. They were both waiting for the opponent to initiate something. Instead, they both locked eyes and paced around the floor trying not to lose focus. The crowd did not understand the lack of action and why both did not fight. They started to cheer, hoping that this would help them. Even Adriana became desperate and started yelling commands to attack. The uncle knew what both competitor's intentions were, so immediately he covered Adriana's mouth, letting her know that her action was unnecessary. What they did not know (both Adriana and the crowd) was that the players were so concentrated that they were looking for the precise moment to confront the other. Time elapsed and they were both still holding onto their own stance without looking away. However, the one who became impatient due to the crowd's cheering was the opponent, so he decided to land a few shots, but without any precision. Martín, on the other hand blocked them without attacking, until he stepped out of line. They both regrouped again and the fighter continued his attack, thinking that his opponent was not going to do the same. Unfortunately for him, Martín performed his signature kick, known as the Mawashi Geri, commonly known as the round kick, which landed accurately on the young boy's face, giving him the point just before the timer expired. This meant that there was no more time to continue and therefore, Martín won the final fight, becoming the champion in his category. What a joyous moment it was; one to keep in the memory vault forever. His dad hugged him and reminded his little ninja that there would be many more championships under his belt.

Nevertheless, that reminiscent dream-bubble did end up bursting the moment that Mo called him useless. Unfortunately for Martín, Mo's discomfort did not stop there, as he was already tired and jealous of seeing this new immigrant having compassion from others. Mo quickly challenged him to a fight during recess after physical education class. Martín did not know what he was getting into, but did recognize that following Mo and the other bystanders was probably not a smart idea. Once outside, Martín was pushed into a circle by one of Mo's friends, and as he turned to see who had pushed him, Mo swung with his left fist landing right above Martín's eyes. Game set match. The fight was over, and the humiliation was more real than ever. Everyone started leaving the circle once they noticed that there was no reaction from Martín, as he stayed on the ground crying, but not so much from the pain (although there was pain) but more so because of the embarrassment he felt deep inside. This truly hurt his ego and his confidence more than the punch itself. No one stayed behind to help him out and once the bell rang, he went inside the school and practically stayed inside the bathroom analyzing his face, especially where the fist landed. He had no time to cry anymore, as he had to quickly invent a story to tell his parents. "They are going to get mad at me" was what kept bothering him. His teacher did not notice him being absent for the last period and therefore did not ask about him, and none of the other students dared bring him up, as they were all scared of Mo and what he was capable of doing. Martín tried covering his goose bump above his head by wearing a hat and looking away from everyone. The moment the bell rang and everyone started being dismissed, Martín exited the bathroom, grabbed his bag, and got lost in the crowd. He immediately left the school.

Walking home he would only think about a story that he needed to fabricate if his parents found out about the bruise he was sporting. The fact that he was once a champion in karate and had received a sucker punch in the face, was making him feel worse than the physical pain. His whole way back home he kept on thinking about why he did not do anything. He even kept on reflecting about the utterance that Mo had said about him. Even though he did not understand what they meant, he still had a good idea of what the message was. His walking commute usually took fifteen minutes, and by the time he got home, his sister and mom would be waiting for him right outside of the building where they lived. This time though, it took him more than twice the amount of time, and that was because he made a few stops; at a playground, at a corner where there was a bench and even by a house that always had a dog outside in the yard. Though he could not see the dog, he always greeted him, hoping that one day, the animal would stop barking. He pondered and pondered what to say to his parents, as he knew that they would immediately notice the moment he took off his hat. As he greeted the same dog and managed to keep him happy (since he could see the wagging tale through the cracks of the one by four fence planks), he felt like he had an epiphany, a solution to his problem; to keep on wearing the hat the whole time and to keep the lights off when it got dark. "What a great idea he thought!" He immediately said goodbye to the dog who had stopped barking and had started wagging his tail. He knew that he was late, and that his mom or even his sister would start questioning his tardiness. As soon as he saw them on the other side of the street and realized that they also had seen him, he sped up to the traffic light. Without noticing a patch of black ice, he spun three hundred and sixty degrees and banged into the post next to it. Fortunately, the post allowed him to keep his composure at the expense of almost hitting his forehead onto the same metal frame. Both his mom and sister crossed the street as soon as it was safe to do and went to see him. His mom took his hat off and noticed that he had harmed his head in the process of his dancing on the ice incident. Right away she did what many moms would do, touch it and press hard against it and ask if he was alright. – Ouch mom, that hurts–, was what Martín immediately and very naturally replied. – Look what you did to your head –, she said. – Let's go home and put some ice on it. Next time do not run on the street. You are lucky that you hit the post and not a moving car. – His mom tended to be a bit dramatic, especially when it had to do with the children getting hurt. This was her way of letting them know of the dangers that are so close by. His sister quickly replied – mom, he's hard headed, he'll be fine. – – Yes, like you– Martín declared.

Once at home, Martín continued checking his bruise every so often, hoping that it would diminish in size as soon as possible. Unfortunately for him, his newly acquired shiner would take more than a couple of days to disappear. He became very aware of the bruise and would continue wearing his hat to hide it away. When his dad came home from work, he realized that Martín had his hat on, so once he gave him a kiss as a part of his greeting, he took off the hat. Suddenly he noticed the bruise and his first words were – who gave you that shiner? – Immediately Martín answered with a negation, but his nervousness implied a different statement than the one that he gave. Having been a psychologist back home, the mom noticed that something else could have happened to her son, not necessarily with the bruise but maybe there was something else that was bugging him. Her motherly instinct allowed her to investigate further, at least about his day, so she asked him questions related to how his day was. Martín continued answering with very quick and short answers, confirming that everything was ok. The mom was able to confirm that there was something or someone that was definitely bothering him.

The next day, Martín woke up earlier than both his mom and sister and decided to go the bathroom to check his face. Once he realized that the bruise was there, he decided that the best thing to do was to not attend school. However, he did not know what to say in order to stay home. Seated by the side of the bath, he continued contemplating a plan, until finally something came to his head. His plan was simple, pretend being sick so that he could stay home. Once he noticed that his mom was awake, he came out of the bathroom holding his tummy. When his mom saw him, he said – my stomach is hurting really bad, mom –. Immediately she grabbed his head to feel his temperature. She strategically placed her hand on his forehead, and both sides of his face, hoping to feel his temperature. She also squeezed his jaw to open it and to check his tongue. She did not notice anything wrong but felt bad for him. She then brought him back to his own bed and comforted him. She continuously asked him if he needed anything, to which he kept on replying with a "no, I just want to rest". Martín was truly tired as the anxiety about what would happen to him at school the next day had disrupted his sleep, sometimes waking him up in the middle of the night. His mom mentioned to him that she would accompany Adriana to school and then come right back to be with him. That was exactly what happened, and the moment that his mom came back, she saw her son sleeping peacefully on his bed. So, she decided not to wake him up to eat breakfast.

That same day soon after the first bell had rung, indicating that school was about to start, one of the Martín's peers accompanied by his parent, went to the teacher to inform him of what Mo had done to Martín, and how Martín had remained in the bathroom by himself while crying. The informant's parent had overheard his child speak on the phone with Mo the same night of the incident, and so had heard how his son and Mo had ridiculed the boy. The father, being infuriated by the action, made his son tell him the full story of the event. Right after that, he took his son to Mo's house to talk to his parents to inform them of what had transpired. Once they both arrived to Mo's house at about seven in the evening, he found out that Mo was alone and unsupervised since there were no parents around. The father left a message for Mo's dad, hoping that he would call him back. He then realized that the dad would never call. Given the severity of the situation (as the father would have explained it), he decided to escort his son to school the next day. Now in front of the teacher, he made his own son declare the truth of yesterday's event. "The teacher felt bad for his new student, especially because he had not seen him that day. Even though Martín was new to the school, he had always come on time. The principal advised him to call Martín's house and to ask his parents about him. So, he did. His call was supported by an interpreter teacher who happened to speak Portuguese and not Spanish, however, was able to convey the message to the mom, given that both Neo-Latin languages have some similarities. The mom found out that her son was punched in the head by this boy right after physical education class. She also found out that her son hid in the bathroom for the last period and as soon as the bell rang, he made his way home. She thought about yesterday and remembered that Martín was about a half an hour late to the house. She also realized that he never mentioned the reason for his tardiness, and then realized that she did not inquire much about it, due to his slip on the sidewalk. She also started questioning whether Martín had banged his head on the post. She then realized that Martín had some explaining to do.

Once he woke up from the slumber, his mom fed him a delicious breakfast, sat by his side and asked him how he was enjoying his new school. He replied that he was happy and that he was making lots of friends. She also asked if he missed home, his friends and relatives. His reply came quickly, assuring his mom that he was so happy to be in Canada that he had no time to really think about his birthplace. She asked about the names of his friends. Taking a couple of seconds, Martín replied with some of their names. Then she asked "Who is Mo?" Martín's face turned red, his eyes opened wide and his pupils dilated. In his silence, he was able to practically confirm the mom's inquiries. She came closer to him and kissed his forehead, beside where the bruise still appeared. Martín's reaction altered the mom, for he started to sob on her shoulder. He could not get a word out, so the mom repeated practically what the teacher had informed her over the phone, to which he nodded assuring the mom that that was exactly what had happened. – Son, I cannot help you out if you don't tell us what is happening. You need to tell us the truth, and right away–, mentioned the mom. Martín assured her by just nodding his head, however, his cry continued still for a few more minutes.

Once he was able to talk, he said, – please, don't tell dad –. – Why do you worry about that? – asked the mom. – Dad will ask me why I did not defend myself? – – Well why did you not defend yourself – asked the mom once again. – I don't know –, he confirmed. He actually knew why he did not fight back. One thing is to fight in a dojo as a sport, in a "one on one" situation, and another was fighting a kid with the home crowd supporting him. In addition, he remembered the teachings of his *sensei*, and that was, to not use karate for fighting, but rather, to defend oneself only in life threating situations. Besides the fact, he could not speak the language, did not know the kids, and did not know the culture. All of these became factors that added to the intimidation that he was already feeling. The one who was once a champion now felt like the laughing stock of his class. He begged his mom to stay home the next day too, but the mom did not succumb to his supplications. She was well aware that he needed to confront this issue and the people that represented it, and not simply to run away and/or hide.

His mom reminded him to practice his karate skills, not necessarily to fight kids, but because she knew that he was the most confident when he practiced this sport. – Son, why don't you practice karate? You had so much fun when you did so! – exclaimed his mom. Martín, although happy to join a sport he was good at, ended up declining the offer, as this sport reminded him so much of his uncle Luchín who had enrolled him in it and did not fly to Canada with him. He had become a second father figure to both Adriana and Martín. In fact, this uncle was very loved by many of the nieces and nephews back home, but it was both Martín and Adriana who ended up being favoured by their uncle's time. This was because Luchín ended up spending a lot of time with these two and even invested in their education. Martín felt like he would be betraying him if he were to join a karate dojo without his uncle being there. – No, mom. No more karate for me and please don't push me to do it anymore. – The mom could not understand where this change of heart from her son was coming from and kept on asking several times without getting a satisfactory answer from Martín. Unfortunately for Martín and for his family, he would not practice this sport again, and the hopes of the parents to see him arise as a prominent karate student disappeared. Their champion had his moment of glory in his own country and here, in Canada, he had to look for another way to stand out.

Chapter 5 – For the Love of Baseball

One month had gone by and Martín still did not feel comfortable with his new peers. He felt like he needed to prove himself every time. This was a very exhausting activity that he did not need, yet felt the need to do so. He pretended to be invisible and sometimes he actually felt like he was doing a formidable job, given that there were days that not even one person would talk to him during class. His teacher did not even ask him to do his work, or ask how he was feeling or even check on his progress.

It was very difficult to get involved in almost anything, as not only was the language troublesome for Martín, but his culture was also different from the Canadian culture. Not to say that he was not happy being in Canada and wanting to become a Canadian, but that, things were different for him. For example, school ended close to three in the afternoon in Canada, whereas, he was used to one thirty back in his country of birth. All learners were supposed to do a lot of group activities, which he was also not used to. For this reason, the pupils needed to meet outside of school to work on a given project. For Martín to have a peer over was something that he was not accustomed to, for he had only had his friends come visit him. His parents would not allow him to visit other kids' homes either, and this was a clear rule. In order for their kids to visit a peer's home, they needed to know not only the friend, but the parents too. His mom and dad were very involved in their lives. In fact, there were times when the parents would accompany the kids to a get together, something that was completely different in their new country. One day a student from his class invited Martín and another friend to his house to work on an assignment that was due the next day. It was imperative for him to be there and try his best to do the work. Martín did not know how to approach his parents on this, as he knew what the answer would be. So, he thought and thought on how to let them know of the importance of the meeting in getting a good grade. Once dinner was finished and he was ready to speak with them, Martín told his parents about his school assignment. His parents looked at each other and suggested for him to have his classmates come over to their home instead. This way, the parents can keep an eye on the activity. Martín did not like the idea, especially as he knew that his apartment was old and it lacked many things, like furniture and even food to offer them. He pleaded with his parents to allow him to go this time and that next time he would definitely suggest to his friends that his house needed to be considered for a school assignment. The parents agreed to his offer under two conditions; that his sister, Adriana, accompany him and be vigilant, and that he would politely ask to use the phone to call them and inform them once they arrived and once they were leaving the place. Martín had no other choice than to accept his parent's offer, if he wanted to go and work on this new classroom assignment.

The moment came when both siblings stood outside of the house of the peer. The dwelling was more like a mansion with big windows everywhere. Adriana stood behind a bay window trying to look in as they both waited for someone to open the door. It took about two to three minutes for someone to finally answer the door and it was the friend who came and allowed them both in, though he was confused when he saw Adriana there. – Me sister, come with me, ok? – mentioned Martín without having enough language to express the reason why she had to come with him. – Okay, whatever –, replied the friend. Adriana asked the boy if she could use the telephone to call home. The boy said sure and pointed to the table where the phone was. After she finished letting the parents know that they had safely arrived, both kids followed the friend down to the basement where there was already the other peer getting his notebook and pencil out to do the assignment. Adriana, was offered a seat with them, but she decided to work on her own homework on a table that was a few feet away from them. She asked about the parents before they got started, and the student mentioned that both of them were working late. Adriana looked at the clock that was hanging on the wall and said – But late. You no eat dinner? –, she commented with her best English possible. – Oh, I ordered pizza and it should arrive at seven. I ordered enough for all of us –, mentioned the boy. – Oh, thank you but we no, because we go home seven. It is late – The boy could not understand why they had to leave so early, as seven o'clock was only an hour away and he knew that their work would take them to approximately that time to finish, plus they needed time to eat. – Anyway –, said the boy – Let's get cracking then –. All three boys opened their math notebook and started working on their answers, Martín was lost, as he had no idea what the word problems were asking. He had good skills for math but the language was impeding him from his comprehension. It took him almost the entire hour to understand the question that the teacher had given the group, but by the time he did so, it was time for them to call home and leave the friend's house. – This is dumb –, exclaimed the other friend, because he was not satisfied with Martín already leaving when the work was not even done. Martín however, understood that he was dumb. His smile quickly left him and he looked at his sister and made a gesture, letting her know that they had to go. She did not hear the boy mention the last remarks that Martín had heard, and for that reason she could not understand why he seemed to be so upset. He did not even give her a moment to ask for the phone to call home, as the parents had asked them to do. They both left the house as the pizza boy was about to knock on the door. The smell of melted mozzarella cheese made him even more irritated since he loved pizza so much and could not even stay for a slice.

By the time they got home (which was a fairly short walk), Martín entered the house and quickly went into the bathroom, avoiding any eye contact with his parents. He did not want to let them know of his struggles, and continued to keep them inside. His sister did not know how to help him. Given that she was a few years older, her struggle with the language was lesser than his. She had a friend who also spoke Spanish. This meant that her friend would interpret and help her during lessons. This friend, like Adriana, was an immigrant. She too left her relatives behind and came to Canada with her brothers and father. She also had a similar upbringing as Adriana. She was very close to her family and like Adriana, she would go home immediately after the last bell to help with the cooking. She introduced Adriana to a few friends who were also Hispanics; some were newer to the country, whereas others had been here for quite some time. They all took turns advising Adriana with school matters, specifically with how teachers were, and which teacher gave the most homework. For her this was interesting, as she used to do this too back at home with her peers. They even graded their educators by the amount of homework they gave, how disciplined they appeared, or even by their looks. In fact, the girls would have nicknames for the most handsome teachers and referred to them (behind their backs, of course) by their nicknames, such as "Hunkie monkey" or "Sugar Cookie Delight" or even "Hot tamale". She liked this and was interested in finding out from her new friends what their pseudonyms were and what they meant.

– Martín, are you ok –, asked his mom. – Yes mom, I just have to use the bathroom –, he replied pretending that he needed to use it, while he shed some angry tears of desperation. Once finished, he sat down on a chair to join the rest of the family for the show they were already watching. His mom patted the empty spot on the same sofa all three were sitting on as a sign for him to sit with them there. At first, he pretended like he did not hear anything but the mom without losing any hope asked him to snuggle with them. He got up and sat with them while showing some type of discouragement. The mom immediately understood that there was something bothering her son but also understood that at that particular moment was not the right time to ask anything. She placed her arm around his back and gently stroked it hoping to transmit her love and affection.

The next day at school, it was time to show the work each group had done. The teacher came around to each group while holding a clipboard. He asked everyone to show their findings. Each group explained their reasoning and how they arrived at their conclusion. Then it was Martín's group. All three boys stood by their work but only the two peers talked about it and then made it clear to the teacher that only the two of them had really worked on this assignment, leaving Martín on the sidelines. The teacher congratulated the two boys, like he did with everyone else, but looked at Martín and showed his disapproval for not getting involved. The poor kid did not know how to tell his teacher that he did go to his peer's house to work on the question. Again, the teacher did not know why this new pupil who had been in his classroom for more than one month would not participate or even do his work. He could not comprehend the lack of interest that he showed. The only thing that he said this time and many other times was "oh well, that's too bad for you, my friend", while leaving him behind to meet another group.

That same day the kids had physical education, which ended up being the first one in a while, since the gym was occupied for almost the whole time that Martín joined the school, and going outside was just out of the question given the crude wintery cold weather. Everyone lined up quietly waiting for the teacher as he took a silent attendance. When he saw Martín, he reminded him that he needed to come in with shorts to class. Although Martín did not understand much of what the teacher was saying, he did recognize the "shorts" message from the teacher's overly loud body language. He understood that the next day for gym, he needed to come with a pair of shorts. And that is exactly what he did; he came to school wearing a pair of shorts for class. His mom reminded him many times that he could not leave the house dressed like that, given that there was a blizzard. – My teacher is going to get mad at me if I do not come to school prepared –, he replied, adding – he told all of us to come to class wearing shorts –. – This cannot be true –, responded the mom. – How in the world would your teacher want you to wear shorts when it is this cold? – –I know–, answered the boy –but I must wear shorts today, so please mom, allow me to do this so that I don't get in trouble –. The mom allowed it but felt bad for her son, as she walked him through the blizzard to get to school. He was the only one wearing shorts, whereas the other kids not only had pants but also had their snow pants on top of the regular ones. Martín felt the cold, and did not want to look at his legs, as this would make him feel the cold even more. His legs were bronzed from the summer weather back at home before arriving to Canada, but by this time they were cracking and dry.

As all of the kids entered the school, Maya left Martín so that she could catch the bus and go to work. Once the homeroom teacher saw the boy dressed the way he was, he just shook his head, showing his discontent once again with Martín. Class continued with no interruptions until another teacher named Mrs. Chan, the new English as a second language teacher came into the room, asking for Martín. This lady was nice and very motherly. She automatically took him to her classroom to teach him language but without overlooking his lack of long pants. She asked him why he came to school dressed that way and he answered "gym". – Oh, you mean you have gym class today? – asked the new teacher. – Yes, gym today. Me go to gym and teacher say shorts –, he replied with some difficulty but less than before. –Oh dear –, she answered, knowing that there was a lack of communication. – Honey, you know that the kids bring a change of clothes when they have physical education. You need to change here, she added. – Martín understood what she had said but also knew that there was no way in the world that he would go to the change room without a teacher there, as the last time that he was there, he was made fun of. She offered him a pair of pants that she had in a bag for kids and said to him to go put them on. If it wasn't because of the bone-chilling cold, Martín would had rejected the idea, however he quickly accepted. This new teacher took Martín to the physical education teacher and told him of what had just happened, and for things like this to not happen again, maybe it was better for her to get involved and help with relaying any message to his house. The teacher agreed, just like the homeroom and the French teachers did too. He mentioned to Martín in a nicer tone (this time) that today they would stay in the gym to play a game of catch. Although embarrassed he simpered, showing for the first time a sense of satisfaction, feeling that this new teacher would help him understand and subsequently, learn English. She took him back to her classroom and showed him a game with a small range of high frequency vocabulary. The idea was for him to match the name to the picture. Then it became a bit more challenging as the teacher asked him to give her a phrase using the word attached to the picture.

She gave him an example, "ball" and said "I play ball". While pronouncing this sentence, she used her gestures, pausing after every word, and made sure to enunciate each syllable clearly, without the need to increase the pitch of her voice. She asked him to repeat the sentence and so he did. Then she wrote the sentence on the board and asked him to write it down. The learning was successfully happening and each time Martín learned something new, she would pat him on the back, smile and tell him that he was doing so well. All of this simply allowed him to feel some hope with the new language. He also felt comfortable and safe and appreciated, especially when she would ask him about his native land. She found out that he was from Peru and brought a book about the Peruvian culture, which allowed Martín to feel important and an expert (although he could not explain much due to the language barrier). Mrs. Chan did not care about him not being able to talk about the book yet, as she knew that the time would come when he would talk endlessly about his country, and explain each page from this book. She knew that for now it was important to focus on comprehension. She knew that learning was not going to happen if there was no comprehension. "How can you learn if you do not understand" would be precisely what she preached. Therefore, she would use her body language, pictures, short sentences and even some Spanish words that she had learned specifically to help Martín. She loved her job so much that it was noticeable in everything she did. This made her very special, particularly for this young immigrant boy, who desperately needed someone to understand him. She made sure that Martín would not misunderstand or be misunderstood by either his teachers or his peers.

That same day the physical education teacher taught the kids a game where they had to catch a soft ball that was pitched by the opposite team and kicked by the other. It was like playing baseball but instead of using a bat, one would use his foot. All the kids enjoyed this game, and in this case, Martín was not the exception. He also realized that he needed to play defense and catch any fly ball in order to get the opponent out. He started becoming competitive and excelling in this game. Martín seemed to be a natural and in the absence of Mo, he felt like he was being accepted by his peers and even by his teacher.

Physical education class ended faster than any of the kids would have loved, even Martín felt that for the first instance that time went by too fast. Although he showed a glimpse of enjoyment in school, his mind still kept on playing tricks, and bringing him back to the past.

Chapter 6 – The Phone Calls

– Hello –, answered the Maya. – *Mi amor*, it's me –, replied Victor, trying to speak loud enough to be heard, as the noise of the traffic in the capital of Panama was overpowering any sort of conversation. This was the first call made by Martín's father, and although he would have loved speaking to the children too, this did not happen, as both kids were in school. The couple however, talked for a short moment and even though it was not enough, it quenched the need that Maya had to hear her husband's voice for the first time since his departure. They chatted enough to find out that he was doing well and that his accommodations were not what was promised, but that it had not changed his mind and turn back, but rather, look forward toward the family's goal. He mentioned to her that Panama was very pretty and warm, and that they had used the pool and the other hotel facilities since that morning. Unfortunately, the hotel did not have phones that made international calls, and for this, he had to cross the street to the nearest payphone to call her. The first time he tried calling, the phone stole his change without allowing him to complete the call. Then after making change from a lunch bill, he made the call that eventually connected him to Maya. He didn't focus on the struggles he encountered but rather on the excited feeling she had in hearing his voice again. It was like winning the lottery. The fact that now she was talking to him felt like he was at work and would come back home soon.

Their talk was sweet and short, but it lacked the enthusiasm that the kids could only bring, and both parents were sad that neither Adriana or Martín had the opportunity to talk to daddy. She asked him if he could call later that evening once the kids were home from their after-school activities, but he mentioned that this might not be possible as the tour guide had mentioned that their travels had to continue that same evening. Maya did not understand, since this was different than the itinerary that was given to them back in Lima. –*Mi amor*, please take care of yourself and do call me back as soon as you can –, pleaded Maya. – But of course, once I am able to call you, I will do exactly that –, assured Victor, momentarily calming her anxious thoughts. The hang up was difficult for both spouses even though the time on the call expired due to the amount of money he had used. She put the receiver down while taking a deep breath in, closing her eyes and thinking of him.

It was the first time that they were separated in two different countries. Her womanly intuition made her feel uneasy and like things were not right. In fact, she felt this way about the trip ever since he brought up the idea. Now she just needed to trust that everything would come to fruition. This was cumbersome since he was not coming back to her. She felt helpless, yet she needed to pull it together so that the kids would not worry. She knew that her worries could easily be transmitted to the Adriana and Martín, making them emotionally unstable. For this reason, she needed to be strong. But at this time, the kids were not home, and she was alone. Therefore, once she placed the receiver back down, she fell on her knees by the foot of her bed and started crying inconsolably. She crumbled in a fetal position while holding onto the pillow that he would have used, letting go of her strengths in exchange for the pain she experienced by not being able to be with her soulmate. It was good that the kids weren't home, for seeing this scene would have affected them too. Her brother Luchín came home roughly an hour after, and was surprised to find her sleeping in bed with a box of paper tissue by her side. He deciphered the situation and deduced that she needed to be alone and rest. He did not wake her up but rather left her to rest and went out to pick up Adriana and Martín from school. Before leaving, he covered her with a blanket she typically used. The exhaustion caused by worrying for her husband debilitated her to slumber a long siesta that she was not accustomed to taking. By the time she woke up, she immediately got out of bed and tried to freshen up although she felt disoriented at first. She realized how late it was and worried about not having picked up the kids, so she grabbed her car keys put on her shoes and started walking toward the door. – Oh, hi mom –, Adriana mentioned. – Hi honey. Sorry I cannot talk… I have to go pick up your brother and you… wait… what are you doing home? How did you get here? – with a blurry mind she asked. – Oh, uncle Luchín picked us up from school –, she stated. – Oh, and what about your brother… where is he? – asked the mom. He is finishing up his dinner, Adriana confirmed. – But I have not cooked yet –, stated the mom all worried about dinner not being prepared. Luchin interjected by saying – Don't worry, sister. I picked up the kids and put together a quick meal. Your dish is in the microwave. Have a seat and I will warm it up for you –, assured Luchín, her brother. – Oh, my goodness… how long was I asleep –, she asked as she lifted her arm to verify the time with her own watch, realizing that she had slumbered for more than three hours. Not believing her eyes and about to get uptight, the brother interjected – just what the doctor would recommend, a good nap! – She looked at him and gave him a smile, showing her satisfaction of having him around to help out with the kids. He did not say anything else but also smiled. It seemed like these two siblings did not need to talk in order to communicate their feelings, as one look in their eyes was enough to transmit their heart's desires. She would be eternally thankful to her brother, and not to mention the kids, since they recalled warm–hearted memories about him numerous times, remembering their fond times together.

Having him around helped everyone in the household. Martín and Adriana had that father figure, while Maya had her younger brother to help her with the house chores and with raising the children. Furthermore, for Martín and Adriana, it was pleasurable seeing their uncle at home. As a matter of fact, when they were small, they would beg him to sleep over and tell them a story about his childhood, or even stay up eating candy, as the uncle would usually do. For these reasons both Adriana and Martín were ecstatic with their uncle being at home. This at least was a diversion from the paramount void they felt due to the departure of their own father, Victor. It was that their uncle had such a way with the nieces and nephews. He knew how to be as friendly as their buddy but still hold the authority without needing to remind them. Although sometimes it was necessary to do so with Martín, especially when his whimsical character got him out of line. Remembering these events brought Martín much bittersweet moments, and if you were to meet him now, he would still feel the same way, even if many years would have passed by.

Maya wanted to tell her kids about their dad calling, but did not know how to do so without breaking their heart. She knew that informing them of a previous call that they had missed would just make them sad. She did not know how to break the ice and waited until that evening when they were seated by the dinner table having a hot chocolate, that she shared the information. The kids reacted in a different way than she had expected, in fact, she was happy that they did not get upset but rather they were happy that mom had spoken with dad. Don't get me wrong, it was not that they did not want to hear his voice but were rather content for their mom, who was able to communicate with her loved one. – Mom, I am sure that dad had done his best to communicate with us –, was what a very mature twelve years old young lady mentioned, without a tone of negativity in her voice. Maya felt much more relaxed, especially after seeing that Martín's face showed the same contentment that his sister had expressed too. – He will call sooner than we can all expect it –, suggested the uncle, trying to maintain the high leveled spirits in the air. Ring, ring, indicated the phone from the kitchen area. All of them looked at each other with awe thinking the same thing but not thinking that it could be true. Martín ran to the kitchen to answer the phone and heard on the receiver an exclamation – *papito* –, by Victor with a cracking voice that tried remaining strong. – Daddy – immediately called out Martín, who tried talking to him for the next three seconds that he could, but his sister yanked the phone off his ear the moment she arrived there. The uncle then took the phone off her and placed it between them both so that they could hear their dad's voice and talk to him. Martín had so much to tell his dad but his sister, being louder and faster with words, was the one able to tell him about her day. Her dad allowed her to talk for a couple of minutes but then reminded her to be kind to her brother and not to cut him out, even if it was accidentally. She promised him that she would be nicer and would acknowledge his needs. Then the dad asked for Martín, who although at the beginning felt an urge to talk to his dad, but by this time his emotions had converted into anger, due to the dad's absence that Martín had interpreted as a form of abandonment. – Honey, pass me to your brother –, he asked Adriana but the moment that he did so, Martín heard these words and decided to run to his room and lie down on his bed, face down. His mom and uncle followed him but the mom did not say anything although she wanted to reprimand him. The uncle touched her on the shoulder and made her aware that this was normal. He suggested her to go back to the kitchen and talk to her husband while he stayed with Martín and discussed his feelings towards his own dad. The uncle had an earful from Martín, and still was able to console him. Luchín stayed with Martín and sat by the foot of his bed, not saying anything but transmitting comfort and understanding via the gentle stroke he did on his back. Maya had gone back to the phone thinking what to say to try to explain to Victor the incident, but happily found that Adriana was doing a great job talking his ear off. Meanwhile, after a few minutes of speaking on the phone, Victor asked for Martín again, and at that moment, before Adriana blurted out what her brother did, the mom took the phone from her and said that he had to run to the bathroom. She lied to her husband because she did not want to hurt him by telling him the truth about Martín's reaction. The spouses chatted for a little while, but as soon as the operator reminded them that there were only fifteen seconds left, they quickly expressed affection for each other, and reminded each other how they would be together very soon. Maya, though she was not a person to wear her emotions on her sleeves, this time she could not contain the tears from coming. Adriana, comforted her by hugging her from behind and once the line cut, she told her that daddy would be ok, and that they would all be together very soon. Maya turned to her daughter, kissed her on the top of her head and told her that she loved her very much. Adriana, then told her mom that she would go and talk to Martín, but the mom said to her – let him be, honey. We all deal with pain differently. Your uncle is with him. – Actually, by the moment she pronounced those words, Luchín came out and mentioned that Martín had fallen asleep, but that they were able to talk for a bit. Maya did not know how to thank her brother for his kindness and his unconditional support, and Luchín was so humble and selfless, never asking for anything in return, or even recognition. He was just happy that he could be of service to his closest sibling.

The next day Victor called again, but this time he was able to grab the phone before any other citizen in the area could. Good thing that he woke up early enough to do this, given that by the time he put his coins in the public machine, there was already one lady lined up behind him and another one coming to line up for the same service.

– *Aló* – answered Maya.

– *Mi amor*, it's me – replied Victor.

– *Hola, mi amor*. I am so glad that you are calling again. Martín was so sad that he could not speak with you yesterday. He is here, let me get him –, mentioned Maya.

– Yes honey, thanks. I called also because I wanted to talk to him –, replied Victor, who had had a feeling that his son was not happy last night, and he wanted to make things better, even if he was far from home.

– *Papá!* – Martín shouted the moment he grabbed the phone, opening his eyes so big to show his profound emotion of happiness.

– Son, I love you so much. How are you? Thank you so much for helping me at home in my absence. You are such a big boy and are helping me by taking care of your mom and your sister –, said Victor.

– *Gracias, papa* –, replied Martín, adding – but I am not doing this alone, as I have the help of uncle Luchín, who is always with us. –

– Yes, I know this and I am so glad that he is there with you guys. Tell me, son, how is school going –

– Well, today is the play at school and mom and uncle are coming to watch. I am sad that you cannot be there daddy. –

– Honey, I am always with you, even if you cannot see me there. I left my heart and soul with you, with your sister and with your mom. There is no distance or time that can take that away. And please don't you forget this, my love –, explained the father.

– Yes, dad... I know this and you don't forget that I love you so much too, even if you don't see me every day. –

– My son, I will never forget this.", assured Victor, allowing a pause in the conversation to let the emotions run their course. "Okay, son, now get ready to go to school. Please pass me your mom so that I can say good bye. –

– Yes dad. Dad, I love you. –

– And I love you with my whole life, my son. Never forget that and sooner than you think we will all be together once again. –

Martín's face showed such amazement and happiness after being able to speak with his dad, and doing so without his sister stealing the phone, all while Victor wiped away his tears and cleared his throat before speaking with his wife. Good thing the lady behind him understood this dilemma and gave him a tissue that she had. He gladly accepted it and thanked her with a smile that communicated tenderness. Both ladies now in the lineup understood the importance of the call and decided to leave and come back later. They both knew that their calls could wait a bit longer. Victor appreciated this kind gesture and showed gratitude by bowing towards them and pronouncing a "*gracias*" without making any sound. Victor and Maya shared their feelings towards each other for a few more minutes until once again the operator reminded them of the fifteen seconds left on the call. They both tried saying how much they loved each other and how much they also missed each other. Maya quickly asked when he would call back but the line cut just as he was answering that his group would be travelling to Mexico via land, that same day. This was a week trip, but by this time, Victor did not know this. It was actually a good thing that he was not able to answer. Unfortunately for the family left behind, they did not receive a new phone call until he reached the English Guatemala, Belize.

Martín would remember his dad's calls very often, especially while being in his new class not understanding a word that his teacher nor his peers were saying. His brain easily took him back to that recollection. His distracted and anxious presence allowed his mind to slide into the past where he would bounce back and forth between emotions of both joy and distress. This time the feeling of not belonging in his new school made him miss his hometown and his family. Once again, he would recall his dad's sporadic phone calls.

It took Victor more than one week to call back, and he did this immediately when he was able to do so, in Belize. He exchanged a few dollars into coins and asked the innkeeper for a payphone.

– *Aló* –, answered uncle Luchín.

– *Hermano* –, replied a very emotional Victor, whose voice was filled with hope yet it kept on cracking, unmasking his nervousness. Luchín was so happy to speak to his brother in-law, (although he considered him more of a flesh and blood brother than anything else) and was also willing to pass the phone to his sister Maya to talk, but for a second he felt like he needed to ask his buddy how he was doing. – It has been a long week of travel. Soon after I called you guys last time, we had to pack our stuff and leave. We were told by the trip facilitator that our hotel room needed to be evacuated due to bugs. This meant that we had just a short period of time to grab our belongings and go to the van that brought us there. Once we had all of the travelers accounted for, the chauffeurs departed. What supposed to be a short ride to another hotel, turned into a journey that took hours. The group leader saw that we, the eight passengers, were so tired and fell asleep, that he decided to continue driving until reaching Costa Rica. I would have called upon arriving but it was in the middle of the night. We stayed in a big house and were given a room with a few beds. We were also reminded that in just a few hours we would meet another driver that would take us to Nicaragua. For the past few days we have been crossing all of Central America until today when we arrived in Belize. I cannot feel my legs or my lower back due to the long drive. They have told us that we will stay here for at least a couple of days, until the van gets serviced. After that we will make our way to Mexico City, where we have been promised our visa to the USA. We have not been given any time to do anything for the last five days. We have slept and even have eaten in the vehicle. We have only stopped for bathroom breaks, for rest and to wash our faces and brush our teeth. The drivers have done their work for twelve-hour shift, but once one ended their shift, another driver would enter the van, allowing the previous one to leave us. The facilitator is telling us that we have to make it to Mexico City as soon as possible so that we do not lose our opportunity of receiving our immigration documents. For now, however, we rest, shower and eat something. –

Luchín was so excited to hear the news but at the same time knew that Victor's departure was a sacrifice not only for the family but also for himself, as he had left everything in order to take on this adventure; all for the family's sake. After speaking for a few minutes, he instantly called his sister letting her know of the unexpected call. Maya came in with her laundry basket ready to be folded but once she found out that her soulmate was on the phone, she accidentally dropped the basket full of clothes. Luchín told her not to worry about it and suggested to continue talking while he would take care of the fallen attire. The couple finally chatted and she was up to date with the information. Unfortunately for them, the kids were both in school and missed their father's call. Victor promised to call back later that day to speak with his kids, and Maya felt appeased knowing that both children would also be pleased to hear their daddy's voice. That same day the happiness was resounding off the walls, especially for Martín, who was literally bouncing off the walls from the fact that his best friend, his *papá*, called again. Although the family did not know when the next call would be (if there happened to be a next one) they felt satisfied that for a moment they had talked to their main man, and trusted deep inside that everything would be ok.

Chapter 7 – The Wintery Month

Gianni and Dani were already in Canada with their parents and were so happy to hear that their extended family was coming also to North America. This particular family had left Peru around the same time that Victor did, with the exception that they came in as visitors and then asked the Canadian government for refugee status. Martín and Adriana were also glad to see their cousins Gianni and Dani, once again. It had been one year since the last time they played together, and the last instance they were together where it also happened to be in a warmer climate. However, in Canada the cold and dry wind welcomed Martín, Adriana and Maya into Canada. Dani showed her excitement to have her cousins by her side, by opening four cans of Coca-Cola, one for each, and served them in glasses, as a gesture of happiness. Martín and Adriana were ecstatic to be able to play together with their cousins who prepared them about the ways in Canada, and about the cold weather (Martín and Adriana had already witnessed and felt it from the moment they left the airport) and about their new school. Unfortunately for them, both families lived in different neighbourhoods, and this meant that they could not attend the same educational institutions. Martín would have loved having a cousin go to school with him, but unfortunately for him, this was not the case. This set of cousins were very close to both Adriana and Martín. In fact, they spent a lot of time together in Peru and even got into trouble plenty of times. There was one occasion when Dani went up on the roof of her house and hopped over to the roof of the neighbour's home, just to have fun. She even asked her cousin, Martín, to meet her up there. Although Martín felt scared of heights and did not want to go up someone else's roof, he felt compelled to do so, thanks to his cousin's persuasive ways. As he made it up (and without any permission), he was told by Dani to remain on the perimeter of the roof. After being up there for a few seconds, Martín felt so empowered, especially because of beating his fear of heights, that he started to walk towards the middle of the roof. The last thing he heard was his cousin's command to go back to the perimeter. However, this command vanished quickly the moment he started falling through a big crack on the laminate roof that he was just on top of. The thin lusterless rusty roof could not contain his weight, making him fall through from the second storey. Thank God that he ended up falling through and landing feet first on the fridge of the neighbour's house, whose members were all congregated on the sofa below, watching television. After falling through and landing on the fridge, Martín checked his body for cuts, scrapes and even bruises and after finding none, he saluted the family below, grabbed an item from the fruit bowl on top of the fridge, climbed back up and quickly scrammed. Both Dani and Martín promised not to say anything and go hide in Dani's room, hoping that no one would know. What they did not expect was that the neighbour waited outside the door for Dani's parents to show them the glassless sunroof above the kitchen that resulted from the fall.

Martín and Dani, spent so much time together that they could write a book about how to get in trouble both in Peru and in Canada.

The snow could not possibly pile up to a higher mountain. Martín had seen glaciers before while taking a flight and crossing the Andes, but he had never seen so much snow at arm's reach. He would say that the pile was ten times taller than him, and that when he would reach the top of one, he could see his new city (although, it was rather more farmland than anything else). "A white cordillera", he called it. He was not sure how snow could amount to such heights, becoming as hard as rock and slippery and cold. This became one of his favourite memories in his new home country. His sister and cousins would climb up these hills with him, and from the peak of the hill, they would make snowballs that they would throw at each other. The rule was simple, to climb to the top and then every man for himself. His clan would spend hours playing in these frozen dunes, and were more excited when they would discover a new peak higher than the ones they had previously mounted.

Playing outside definitely helped him acclimatize to the weather and the elements fairly quickly. It seemed like it was always cold, but the fact of the matter was that he had arrived during the winter, and unfortunately for him (and his family), those first four weeks were historically one of the worst in years. Fortunately, his demeanor and young age helped him see and appreciate this cold wave. His mom on the other hand, would feel like walking icicles whenever outside, not anticipating that the cold could get any colder. "It was just not possible", they would say… but it was. For the parents, it felt better to stay inside their apartment during what they considered the "ice-age" and not go outside, unless it was truly necessary. For this reason, they did not enjoy the wintery wonderland and the activities that people would participate in. In fact, for the parents, it felt crazy to freeze one's rear while being outdoors. For them the idea of being outside was painful and futile, and therefore saw it as a complete waste of time. Maybe because of the lack of good quality winter attire, and also because they had to wait for the bus during wind-burning gusts that would freeze the tiny hairs in their nose (a feeling that they had never experienced before). Adriana and Martín nevertheless could not be bothered by the cold of the season. Even the grey days or the deceiving sunny days would not keep them inside. This was something that the parents needed to accept; the fact that they were still kids and wanted to experience the winter and play outside.

There were times however, that even Martín and his sister felt the cold to their inner core, and instead of complaining, it was customary for Adriana to think of the past. She immediately would evoke a warm sentiment once lived. In this case, she remembered the times that they would go to the beach year-round. Their home city did not have strong winters like here, and therefore, it was natural to go visit the waves at any given time. There was one beach that his whole family would visit frequently. This one was very particular, and some even would have considered it peculiar, due to the fact that it did not have a sandy shore like the ones nearby. In fact, it was all soft and smooth greyish blue stones, with smaller pebbles closer to where the water would filter back into the ocean. During a hot sunny day, it was very common for people to hop barefoot in pain over the stones, due to the heat embedded in these nuggets. Some people would laugh at others, as they tried walking unshod to the water from their own seating area. But then it was their turn to do the same, and at that time they would not laugh, but rather feel the same pain. Their eyes gave them hope, once they would fixate them on the delicious and inviting Pacific salty waters. It was all well worth it once their body was submerged in crystal clear cool-to-the-soul water. You would just take a deep breath and then suck in the aroma of salt, fresh fish and seaweed. If going swimming makes people go hungry, smelling delicious food from a nearby restaurant would just have you salivate until you are finally in front of your favourite dish.

The family would enjoy their time together by the sea, and although they did not have water toys, except for the occasional beach-ball, the waves would help them stay entertained, especially when a strong one would come and push someone on to the hot stones. At times, the family would go back to the semi humid stones and instead of building sand castle as there was no sand there, they would excavate in search for crabs. If they dug deeper into where there was water, they would also find fish, shells, spiders and other aquatic colorful creatures. Together with a bucket they would collect certain "pets" that would accompany them while being at the beach, but later were released back to their natural habitat.

Beach visits were all day long, and Adriana and Martín would beg their parents to stay back until the sunset, as it always happened in the horizon, showering the sky with vivid purple, pink and yellow hues. All four remained motionless seated on top of the pebbles whilst enjoying their last scene before packing it in. The warm feeling of the last few rays, accompanied by the pleasant water trickling above their rubbery sandals, would culminate a joyful family gathering.

Martín would also remember another water event; one that he did not live but rather heard from his dad, and that was the times when his dad was submerged under water trying to cross the Mexico-US border.

Their new home in Canada was not far away from water. As a matter of fact, the grandiose lake was just a few kilometers away. They thought that it would be fun to visit it for the day. Though they had never done so, they knew of its whereabouts as they looked south and saw the horizon. A friend that they had met shortly after their arrival, who also had a vehicle, took the family to this part of town known as the "Lakeshore". It was quite phenomenal to be able to see ice on the lake and strong waves hitting the big rocks and once splashing all over the boulders, would tame the waters, keeping it in its place. Very quickly the family became enamored with the scenery. They kept on calling the body of water the ocean and could not understand how this could only be a lake. The size of it simply mesmerized them, inviting them to stay awhile, enjoy a picnic or even a barbeque. However, the nippy weather reminded them to go back to the car and put an end to their first outdoor Canadian adventure. Too bad for Adriana and Martín, who wanted to continue enjoying and exploring the great outdoors. Adriana understood that the cold was overpowering and unbearable for their parents and quickly reminded Martín that it was time to get going. She grabbed her brother by the shoulder and shepherded him back to the car where the parents were seated under a thick wool Peruvian blanket, sipping their hot Tim Horton's coffee. It seemed like the coffee revitalized their spirit, allowing them to feel their toes and fingers once again. The kids however, showed their discontentment for leaving so early, yet understood that the cold was too strong for people to be outside. At the end, the driver-friend promised the kids that he would bring them all back whenever it got warmer. This ignited up a smile in the kids who finally accepted the fact that it was truly very cold.

The next day was a school day and Martín was accompanied by his mom to school. Maya wanted to come to pay closer attention to what was going on with her son and the other kids. She did not know how to explain herself to any of the teachers, given that she did not speak a single word of English, but decided to drop him off every morning. – This at least will be an opportunity to observe any strange behavior with Martín –, thought the mom. However, she recognized that this really may not be helpful, given that kids usually misbehave either behind closed doors, or when an adult is not watching or in the vicinity. At the same time though, Martín was usually not bothered by most of the kids, which was always a good thing. – Hey Martin, are you coming to the baseball tryouts in the gym? – asked his friend Richard the moment he saw Martín with his mom. While Martín did not understand the full message, he was able to decipher baseball and gym, as these were two of the words that he was coming to know. Richard continued explaining with gestures and by repeating certain key words to help Martín understand. Maya then put the pieces together and realized that this young lad was inviting her son to a sports tryout, so, she decided to explain in their native tongue. – Ah yes, me like –, replied a very excited Martín. – Well then, I will come and get you at lunch time –, exclaimed Richard, while patting Martín on the back. Maya felt comfortable leaving her son at school and thought that there would be no more issues. Yet the moment she left was precisely when Mo came by with his crew. – You can't tryout, dummy 'cause you are stupid –, yelled Mo to Martín. Mo's group quickly broke off and surrounded Martín from all four corners, pretending to dissuade him from trying out. Nevertheless, the bell could not have rung at a most opportune time, making all of the kids line up while their teachers came out to greet them and to bring them inside.

The afternoon came, and so did lunch time. While the majority of kids went outside for recess, Richard met Martín outside the classroom. He then grabbed him and took him into the gym. It seemed like Richard also carried the excitement of the two of them in the gym, while the anxiety was also clearly seen in Martín's face. Once in, he noticed that the other participants were in partners tossing a tennis ball while catching it with their appropriate glove. Suddenly Mo came in with his partner and called out "Martín". After doing so, he whipped the ball against Martín who was not too far away from him and who was also with his back turned towards Mo. Thank God, that Richard's cry calling out for Martín's attention allowed Martín to quickly turn around, move

74

out of the way and extend out his hand and catch the sphere that was about to land in his face. Everyone was in awe, as they witnessed one of the best catches ever by a feline-like lad. Even the coach saw this and showed great satisfaction, thinking that Martín would be a great asset for the team that he was trying to build. As for Martín, once he grabbed the ball he looked at Mo directly in the eye, walked towards him and while saying "nice throw", he granny tossed the ball back to him. Mo, although perplexed considered this action to be honorable and felt like he was taught a lesson. His friend then mentioned that Martín would be good for the team and Mo agreed even if he did not say it out loud.

The tryout went well and there was a lot of hype from all of the participants. The coach worked on catching pop flies and grounders. The activity was limited due to being inside the gym but it at least gave the kids a few activities to focus on, and to pick the ones for the team. There were two coaches. One was the physical education teacher and the other one was a parent volunteer, who happened to be a coach for a summer league team. Many kids made the team but two stood out, one for his intelligent playmaking and the other one for showing a high degree of interest accompanied by some ability, though his talent was like that of a diamond in the rough. (You might guess that the first kid was Mo and that the second one was Martín, and you would have hit the nail right on the head.) At the end of the practice, the coaches asked the kids to sit in front of them while they would read the names of the chosen players. Mo was the first one to be called and Martín was the last one, and in between, there were sixteen more. All of the kids who made the team showed their excitement and left the gym with glory in their arms, while the ones empty-handed were crestfallen.

The tryouts and the new team was what many kids in Martín's class talked about. Good thing that the teacher understood the excitement, and therefore, allowed it. However, he had to put an end to this, when he noticed that two of his kids did not make the team and seemed very sad. Luckily, the second part of the day went by very fast and soon it was time for dismissal. When this happened, Martín grabbed his language notebook and his homework, placed it in his bag and started walking out. Once out, he realized that Mo was walking ahead of him, so Martín decided to wait a few more minutes until he could not see Mo anymore. He considered himself safe once Mo was not able to see him if he happened to turn around. Though Mo had shown a glimpse of satisfaction towards him, Martín still did not feel comfortable walking with him or behind him.

His walk home was as normal as always, but this time there was something peculiar about it. Martín noticed that there was noise of a fight coming from a house near him. He got scared and his instincts made him hide behind a bush of a neighboring house. From there he noticed that a man was yelling profanity to someone who was also screaming. It must have been a kid, given that his voice was cracking and very thin. Martín got scared and continued behind the bush. The commotion continued with the slamming of the door followed by more insults from the adult. Martín was right, since he saw that there was a kid who was the one fighting with the adult. What he did not assume was that that kid was Mo. He saw Mo run out of the house, also screaming and yelling back to his dad, using some kind of angry language that Martín did not understand the meaning of message, although the intention seemed crystal clear. He then got scared for his classmate and did not know what to do. Suddenly, he saw Mo pick up a basketball from his front yard and toss it with all of his strength against what seemed to be a window, for the shattering of broken glass was so loud that it really scared Martín. Mo ran out away from his house while Martín came out of his hiding place. He was perplexed and terrified, since he had never witnessed a father and son fight, especially to this caliber. He started to walk away from the bush and as he passed by the house, he noticed the broken glass of the front window. He also saw Mo's dad, who had also come out wearing a white tank top and ripped blue jeans while holding a drink in his hand. Again, he heard the same type of vocabulary, that was once said by both father and son. The man asked Martín "what you looking at, kid?" and Martín instead of replying, ran faster than he had ever done so before, disappearing as fast as he could. Faster than the cold breath that spouted out of the father's frail and cold body.

For the first time, he was saddened for Mo. He could not understand how a father could treat his son in such an ill manner. He automatically started thinking of his dad, and how his dad sacrificed so much for his own family. He immediately evoked another memory that his dad had shared…

The water was cold and the smell of waste and dead flesh was in the air. Good thing it was dark, and the reflection of the moon which guided them, did not allow the travelers to see the horror at their feet. People had to be quiet and move slowly while following orders from the man known as the "coyote". He would lead the pack to the other side, ever so quietly, without making more noise than the floating waters cascading into the rocks below. With a slight move of hand above the river, he would direct the silent group of men, women and kids to safety. Of course, this was not as easy as it sounds, as there were at least two or more helicopters roaming above the grounds, shining their bright light from above and down below to the terrain and stream, looking for illegal aliens who were eager to get to the other side. The water was cold, like the air above, and the rocks were slippery and unstable. The kids were holding onto their moms for dear life. Some of them would be carried on their parent's back. Two little girls were doing the same on Victor's back, who although was forty years old, by this time felt the strength of a water buffalo. All of the kids had one thing in common; their eyes were fully shut. This actually helped them not get scared. The adults however, took on a level of valor and strength, not coughing or shivering from the cold, nor showing any signs of faintness from the trajectory. Instead they all united in strength and guided each other to safety.

This was the closest that the group had worked together. It seemed like they had learned to leave behind their differences. This was not the case all the time however, as there were many arguments and even fights throughout their time. In fact, when they left Belize, a young man, in his late twenties named Carlos boarded the bus that would take them to Mexico City. This man was tall with a strong frame, dark features and curly hair, and from the moment he came on the bus, he started treating everyone with disrespect, as if he were setting the tone or marking his territory. No one accepted this type of behavior, yet he continued talking to people with ignorance and arrogance. He would approach the ladies with a seductive and sly behavior. None of the females felt comfortable being close to him but none of them were outspoken enough to let him know that his remarks and advances were not welcomed. Nonetheless, he did not care and would continue his dirty scheme towards all of the women.

During their travel to the Mexican-United States border, everyone on the bus was fatigued and fell asleep, with the exception of the women, who felt extremely uncomfortable being around Carlos. With the men "out of commission", he continued his seduction, once again. Victor, who was a light sleeper happened to awake from a startling commotion. It was a woman distraught and struggling with Carlos. Victor had enough, got out of his chair, grabbed Carlos from behind the collar and placed him back on his own seat. – If you try this again with her or any of the other women, I will come after you. You understand? – communicated a hyper Victor to a less excited Carlos. That woman, still scared and with an agitated breathing, looked at Victor, and although did not voice anything, her eyes let him know that she was very thankful. Once Victor received her message, he went back to his seat. He sat down but this time facing Carlos' way, hoping that he would not try anymore dirty work on this woman or on anyone else. Carlos, however, felt like he had lost the battle but not the war, and was hoping to try again, when all of the men were finally "unavailable".

The small bus tried crossing the border before the river scene but there was an unfortunate event that stopped it from doing so. During their first time, the bus left the motel with more people than seats available. Some of them were lying on the ground and between the seats. The women and kids had the chairs, whereas the men had the ground. The drive to the edge of the border was a couple of hours away, but the uncomfortable situation, made it seem like it was a lot longer. The guide took time at the beginning of the trip to notify everyone of the plan and how it would be executed in order to not be caught by the immigration officers in the US. Once he did so, he sat down beside the driver and everyone started falling asleep. Carlos thought that this would be the best time to continue his move on one of the ladies on the bus. He decided to prey on a young girl who happened to be seated on the bench adjacent to him. He quickly started harassing the girl and even though she complained, it was not enough for him to stop his advances. So, he continued with the wrongful actions. The girl felt afraid and overpowered by him, hence, did not know what to do. Thankfully, Victor who happened to be a few isles away from this, opened his eyes automatically and noticed what was about to happen to this young girl. Somehow, he leapt from his seat and flew what seemed to be ten feet and landed on top of the tormentor. Victor did not care for the consequences, and could only think of the safety of that young girl. He quickly latched on to Carlos' back, threw him into the ground where there once laid someone else, and started pounding him. As he did so, he yelled – I told you to stay away from the ladies. I told you that if you happened to touch one of them, that I would come after you? – Every sentence or phrase he said to Carlos was followed by a blow. Suddenly, Carlos exclaimed – let me go, or we are going to die –. This however, did not stop Victor from the action, and continued punishing him for his wrongdoings. – Please, let me go… the bus is on fire –, cried out a very petrified man. Finally, Victor stopped the blows, looked up and noticed that the bus had caught fire and that no one was on it except Carlos and him. He heard the screams from all of the passengers, telling them to jump out of the bus before it exploded. Thank heavens that Victor got out of the trance that dominated him for the past five to seven minutes, grabbed Carlos by the neck and threw him off the bus. He then jumped out into the small hill where everyone was congregating. Shortly after he did this, the bus exploded.

Thank God no one was hurt with the exception of Carlos, but not because of the fire or explosion, rather due to the pounding he took on just before. Everyone hugged each other giving thanks to God for not having suffered any major loss, although they did lose many of their belongings. Carlos, who had looked death in the eye, started to weep like a baby once the adrenaline settled down. No one felt like helping him out especially after what he had done. However, Victor grabbed his hand, helped him get up from the ground and reminded him to stay away from all of the ladies on the bus. Carlos immediately nodded his head as a sign of agreement and followed the crowd, who was in the middle of a deserted, dark, and gloomy road. Everyone was waiting for the guide to let them know what would happen next and what the immediate plan would be, but neither the guide nor the driver really knew what to do. So, they all decided to come close together and sleep side by side. Victor and another man made sure to sleep on both sides of the perpetrator, Carlos, to keep a close guard on him. It was close to ten in the evening and everyone fell asleep until the first ray of the eastern sun showered them with hope, once again.

At times, it felt like the current of the river was stronger, and when this happened, the people grabbed onto each other so that no one fell. They also knew that if one was caught, all of them would be too. The walk was longer than expected and when they finally made it to the other side, they would hide in the bushes that the terrain graciously offered. The cold reminded them that they were wet. Nevertheless, there was nothing that could be done with this respect. The good thing was that the kids who were carried on the shoulders of the others, only had their legs and feet wet. Nonetheless, it felt like the children had matured tremendously during this voyage given that they did not complain at all. They were just thankful to have made it to the other side. The "coyote" then mentioned to all of them that he would be going back across, once their contact reached them and took them to a nearby home. It did not take too long for this to happen as the help came in faster than expected. In fact, the help was anticipating the group to cross a few hours prior, but understood that this type of work needed not to be rushed otherwise it could fail. Once the new guide came over, he greeted them with a quiet gesture and led them through a long walk across the desert towards a house belonging to a Central American family. All thirty voyageurs were tired and could only think of going to sleep. The emotional distress was huge and the long walk and the cold water also fatigued them to a point of non-function. No one cared to take off their wet and cold clothes, however, the owner of the house had prepared clean clothes for all of them, including the kids. The rule that the owner had was that everyone needed to take a two-minute shower, put on the provided clothes, eat and then rest up, knowing that the next day was their time to depart and go their own ways. The newcomers were all thankful to the family for allowing them to stay, eat and warm up. They finally felt like they had made their American dream come true. Well, all of them but one shared the same sentiment. Carlos on the other hand had a sense of superiority and acted very condescending towards everyone in the group. He thought that because he had lived in the United States of America, before being deported, he was better than everyone else. Good thing that no one cared and did not allow his demeanor to overshadow their joy. What everyone had in mind was to reach their final destinations. Places like New York, Los Angeles, Detroit and other places to meet their respective family, get a job and bring over their spouses and kids. This was the same thought for Victor, who by now had forgotten the struggles of a six-month period from the last time he saw his family until now. He knew that it had been two weeks since he had spoken to them and could only think of calling the next morning. He could anticipate the conversation with his wife, Martín and Adriana, and had tears of excitement gathering in the corner of his eyes. He knew that his wife would have a million questions to ask, and he needed to tell her everything without worrying her with the negative details. He started thinking about what to say and what to omit. Suddenly he fell asleep and his brain blacked out completely, allowing him to finally get a good night's rest.

Chapter 8 – The Next Phone Call

The next morning came faster than expected. Although Victor had a good night's sleep, similar to everyone else, he felt as if he could have slept for a few more days. It seemed like this was everyone's sentiment as well, and the homeowners were prepared for this. For that precise reason, they made sure to make their guest feel welcomed and safe, not mentioning a time for departure. They had also gone through the same process before legalizing their status in their new country. They knew the pains, sacrifices and long haul all of them had undergone. They also noticed in Victor's eyes a shadow of sadness that they did not fully understand, especially after his accomplishment of crossing the border the previous night. Once Victor got up and got ready, he went to the kitchen and saw both owners preparing a hearty breakfast. After greeting them and thanking them for the accommodations, he washed his hands in the kitchen sink and started helping out, without asking permission. Both owners thought that this was very honorable and thanked him for his help. Victor, looked at them and showed his satisfaction with a smile. This is when the wife noticed that there was still something perturbing him, and therefore, decided to be upfront and ask what the problem was. Victor mentioned that he had a wife and two kids, and that they had stayed behind at home, with hopes that he would make it to the United States. He also mentioned to them that it had been six months since his parting and a couple of weeks since they last spoke. Both husband and wife, owners of the house, looked at each other and said to him that they had something for him. Quickly the husband took Victor by the arm to an office that only had a desk, a typewriter and a telephone. He pointed at this last device and said "go ahead". Victor, though perplexed for a second, deciphered the message, thanked him and went about a phone call.

– *Aló* –, said Martín the moment he answered the phone call. – *Hijo* –, called out the father on the other line. – *Papá*, I miss you so much! Where are you now? When are you going to make it to the US? When are we meeting you there? I want to see you. It's been too long since we last saw you, *papá*. We all miss you lots. – There were a few queries and statements mixed with sorrow and anxiousness that a very excited Martín was able to articulate until his dad started answering each of them, one by one. He then told his son that they would soon be together and that he had finally made it. The son screamed an over-the-top animated cheer, with which he attained everyone's attention in the house, who happened to run towards him. Although Maya rhetorically asked if that was Victor on the line, she had a feeling that he was. Both, she and Adriana, decided to get closer to the receiver, placing their ear on each side of Martín's head, in order to hear the conversation. Victor, knew how important the conversation was for his son, that he decided not to ask for his wife, and knowing that all three of them were glued to the phone (he heard the ladies' excitement), he continued answering the questions that were asked primarily by his son. Their conversation was full of emotions, joy, tears and more happiness, but due to time already spent on the call, Victor reminded them that he had to hang up promptly. During their talk, he brought the family up-to-date, mentioning that he was finally in California, in the house of a couple of angels. Maya asked Victor to thank the couple on her behalf, and just like the kids, sent a million kisses his way. Victor said that he had received all of the kisses and that he had placed some in his pocket, to use later that day and until the next time they would talk again. He also mentioned that he had plans to travel to New York, to meet his extended family and to try to establish his life there. He then assured his wife that their sacrifice was not in vain. She agreed and said that she could not wait until the next time they would talk to each other in the same room. – It will happen sooner than you expect it –, he assured her. The kids told their dad that they loved him and as soon as this sentiment was received, Adriana took her brother back to the living room, allowing her mom to have a private second with their dad. Maya then met their kids in the same room a short instance afterwards, with a smile that would have lit any room in the house.

After hanging up the call, Victor, went back to the kitchen where the couple continued the meal, and he helped them with the preparations. He continuously thanked them for their kind gesture. The wife had mentioned to him that it was a very short call for a man that had not seen his family in "ages" (of course she was exaggerating, but still understood that even one day away from your loved ones can feel like an eternity). She did not want to pry in Victor's life but showed interest in his life and that of his family. Victor had no reason for not trusting the couple and began to share his story from the moment all four family members were gathered in the US embassy early in the morning.

The conversation ended the moment when the other trekkers joined them in the kitchen, offering their help by setting the table. – This is a tough journey –, mentioned the husband to Victor, while holding on to Victor's shoulder, and expressing his sincerity. His wife on the other hand wore her emotions on her sleeve and uncovered a few tears. Victor's story had touched her heart, and she could feel the family's pain by the separation, the anxiety and distress. Her dad had done the same journey as a Guatemalan native a few decades ago, and although the adventure was not as dangerous as now, she witnessed her mom enduring the same pains at home with five tiny mouths to feed. She not only felt, but ached for what all of these guests had to suffer in order to achieve the so called "American Dream".

The breakfast was full of exquisite and delightful treats. There were eggs cooked in different ways, a batch full of pancakes, a big bowl of fresh cut fruit, and what seemed a platter of bacon, sausages and fried plantains. It was definitely a culinary fusion of two types of foods; from the north and the south. No one could believe their eyes, being so thankful for the provisions. Then the homeowner reminded her husband of the breads, so he went to the kitchen and brought over to the table different kinds of doughy delights, including the famous flatbreads that Mexicans call "tortillas". The food was plenty, and although hunger existed in the faces of all of the travelers, it only took so little to satisfy their need. The husband understood that due to the long journey and with little nourishment available for them all, their stomachs had shrunk in size and would only accept small doses of food at a time. Everyone was satiated. Following one by one, they started thanking the couple and saying their goodbyes, as if they already knew where they were going. In fact, most of them already had plans to travel either by plane or by land to their final destinations where their relatives were already established. Everyone thanked the couple for their hospitality and started off on their ways. Both the homeowners were glad to have been helpful to everyone in the house. They knew the feeling first hand and relived it with the new group that stayed in their house.

The moment came when it was time for Victor to leave also. He gathered the small amount of extra stuff he had, placed them in a plastic bag he had received from one of the homeowners and put on his jacket, which by this time, was already dried out from when crossing the river. He thanked both proprietors with a handshake. However, the husband after receiving his hand, pulled him over and gave him a big hug. The wife also joined in and reminded Victor that soon his family would be here with him. – Please keep in touch and if you need anything, just let us know. – – Thank you for being so attentive to all of us, and for allowing me to speak to my family –, he mentioned. Victor left very happy to have met this new family and started counting his blessings for having made it to North America.

Victor never got the opportunity to talk to that couple from California again, but had such sentimental regards for them that he would share it with many people. During his flight to New York, he kept on thinking about his family, and how he needed to look for a job immediately, in order to send money home. He knew that not having worked for a few months would have had a negative effect on the family's economics. Good thing that a relative in New York found him a local job in the supermarket where he himself worked at. This allowed the family at home to survive the tough times of rotten finances.

In Peru, the family was overjoyed knowing that their loved one had made it. The kids particularly, started counting down to a possible date that they thought would be the next time they would see their dad. The timing of Victor's arrival to the "Home of the Free" could not have been more opportune for the whole family and also the moment he landed in his cousin's house, he started working, which meant that he could send money to his family. The situation back in Peru had gone from bad to worse in matters of weeks and the providence from Victor was favorable for the entire family. When the cash advance company called Maya to let her know that there was an amount of funds sent to her, she could not stop giving thanks. She knew that it had come from her husband but was not expecting any monies anytime soon, and for this, she was very appreciative. -Any help during this time of need, was welcomed-.

Chapter 9 – The New "Extended Family" in Canada

Martín, Adriana and their parents went on a road trip with an older couple that had recently met them at their arrival destination in Canada. Fenny and Horace had been married for a few years and were also immigrants from South America, but had been in Canada for a couple of decades already. They were well established and had a heart of giving. They also had a car, and had offered to take the newcomers to a town called Orillia; a couple of hours away from their new home. This was well received by everyone in Martín's family, as they wanted to get to know their new country. The couple simply took them in as family, and soon they seemed to have become one. In fact, their friendship grew so much that until now they are still connected.

Fenny met Victor first, the day she went to pick up her husband Horace from English-as-a-Second-Language night school. Coincidentally Horace was also attending the same school to perfect his language skills. As usual, she waited in her car for Horace to finish. She saw Victor outside the building smoking a cigarette. She then saw him walk towards the bus stop across the street, where he waited for the next shuttle to take him home. Fenny did not do anything but just watch this younger man. Once Horace came into the car, Fenny asked her husband if he knew that man. The sadness in Victor's eyes caught Fenny's attention. Although there was poor lighting from a few fixtures outside in the parking lot, Victor's facial expressions of loneliness were illuminated enough to show everyone his fatigued soul caused from a heavy day's work in addition to the longing he felt for his family. Fenny asked Horace once again if he knew him, and he replied that they both were in the same class learning English. Unfortunately, Horace had not had the opportunity to talk to him, as the class got divided into two groups that same day. Victor's group left with another teacher not having allowed Horace to have the opportunity to introduce himself. He also mentioned that it was the first time that Victor had come to class. Fenny paid close attention to what her husband was saying, but also felt that she had a mission to fulfill, and that was precisely to befriend that man she considered a lost soul. She drove towards the bus stop and asked Horace to go talk to him. At first Horace declined the idea, mentioning that he was tired and just wanted to go home to get ready for bedtime. Fenny would not drive away and after a few worded battles with her husband, it was she who ended up parking behind the bus stop, and coming out of the car where she introduced herself in Spanish. – *Hola, amigo...* how are you? – asked Fenny. – Hi lady– replied Victor also in his native tongue, not trying to be short in his response but the weariness in his eyes, along with the exhaustion, would not permit him to show more emotions. This plus the fact that it was a stranger coming out of a car with a man, made Victor feel bit worried. – My name is Fenny, and the man inside the car is my husband. His name is Horace. He is in your English class. He mentioned that he saw you there today. Can we give you a ride to your house? The bus you are waiting for, usually takes about an hour or close to it, to arrive. – At first, Victor did not know what to say, as he was on guard, even though the lady in front of him presented herself very peaceful and genuine. But the idea of getting into a stranger's car was something that he had never done, and now in his early forties, he was not going to make this mistake. Horace noticed the man's resistance and lack of conversation with his wife, so finally decided to come out of the co-pilot's seat and introduce himself. Sometimes the presence of another man makes the situation more confrontational. However, in this case Horace's positive and friendly demeanor made Victor trust in the couple's intentions, hence agreeing to get into the car and graciously receive a ride home.

What happened next is that through this couple Victor saw and felt a true conviction of faith, hope and love through the willingness Fenny and Horace displayed in serving their neighbours. He felt extremely comfortable with them and over a short period of time and frequent future visits, either at the school's parking lot, Fenny and Horace became like Victor's older siblings. Horace had the opportunity to ask Victor to his house for some food and a coffee afterwards. It is true what they say that food usually brings people together. However, in this case, it was the solidarity and the attention to serve, that truly hit deep into Victor's heart. There were many times that Victor would feel the absence of his loved ones, making his spirit wretched and desolate. Not knowing when he would see them again, made his soul feel unrested. He however, noticed a "Divine Hand" interceding and placing the right people on his path, for a reason. This gave him comfort and tranquility, changing his attitude to a more prospective and with a future to prosper and to give him hope. Now, with a new set of friends like Fenny and Horace, Victor felt comforted and hopeful. He would even talk about them to his own family back in Peru, and the couple was so excited to find out when the rest of the clan would come to Canada, so that they could help them and guide them in a new country. It seemed that this couple knew the struggles that new immigrants generally underwent, and for that reason they wanted to be useful and serve others. To this day, Victor's family is still in contact with them, and Martín and Adriana consider them grandparents.

Victor quickly noticed the intentions Fenny and Horace had. That was to share and to show affection which in turn would help ease any struggle that an immigrant underwent. Finding a group of people that can ease the burden (of being a newcomer) can help one acculturate more rapidly and efficiently. Victor would frequently compare his personal and taxing experience crossing the Americas with the one to Canada. He felt like God was watching over him, and Fenny and Horace were there to confirm this truth, over and over.

Their visit to Orillia was more than what they expected. Some of the trees were still covered with cotton-like snow, while others were completely naked, having been defoliated a few months prior. In the car and on the whole way to Orillia you could hear Maya comment how beautiful the trees looked, regardless of their shape, condition or size. Martín and Adriana remained glued to the one window they both shared, taking turns brushing their nose onto the glass. For them this was food to their souls and music to their ears, being able to enjoy such majestic views with the presence of their daddy. It had been a month now since they were first united at the airport. In fact, that day was as sweet as honey for Victor, but rather bitter-sweet for Martín and Adriana. That is, because, the union to their father meant leaving behind an entire community of relatives and friends that had helped them all during the time that Victor was absent. Some of them, such as their uncle Luchín meant the world to them both. With the departure of their daddy, they received the father-like figure by being there always. While gazing outside (from his seat) at the beauty of God's creation, Martín started missing his relatives once again. He relived numerous events. Nevertheless, the one that was still fresh in his mind was this...

The night of the departure to Canada, Martín's family received an army of beloved people in their house, as they started trickling in from early afternoon, all the way until the last minute prior to departing from their home. Some people decided to say their good byes early enough, anticipating that the house would be full with relatives and friends, as the time approached "D-time". Precisely this is what happened. Even Victor's coworkers came to say their goodbyes. The day came and went, similar to Victor's departure. Martín, although thrilled to see his daddy once again, was reminiscing on the fact that very shortly he would not be able to see his uncles again. The thought was painful, especially after having three very devoted uncles support them financially and emotionally. He felt torn, yet the excitement of seeing his dad after more than a year soothed his soul. "We will be together again" was what entered his mind, finding a way to comfort him. His uncles would remind him that soon they would see each other again. The impact that a caring adult or family member has over a child is invaluable. For this reason, it is important to seek these situations as a loving adult, that is, to make a difference in the life of those who need it, especially when they are newcomers and have left their heart behind. That moment came when a caravan filled with people proceeded to the airport. Maya could feel the support from everyone, and as always, her charismatic way shone to such a degree that would also hide her sadness for leaving a multitude of loved ones behind.

It was uncle Luchín who had permission to accompany the family all the way to the airport's gate. He was allowed to stay with his sister and the kids for an extra hour, until it was time for the three to board the plane. Their time was spent talking, telling jokes, reminiscing on their anecdotes and finding a way to see each other in the near future. Finally, the call was made, asking all of the passengers to board. Maya looked at her younger brother and with teary eyes, gave him a smile that was obscured by the sadness painted in her depth. Both the kids gave him a hug before boarding, with Maya mentioning to him that the distance will never allow her to forget him or abandon him. She was grateful that he had given so much of himself to help her and the kids. She was so thankful. Anyone viewing this picture would tell you that the departure was sad like they usually are, but what Luchín would tell you was that he was content to know that the three would be reunited with Victor once again.

Martín and his family had taken many flights before, but none of them were as long and as turbulent as this one to Canada. The hope was that they would sleep during the overnight flight, and wake up just before the landing. Nonetheless, the bumpy and windy ride made it nearly impossible to have a proper shuteye. Anticipation was making it even worse to fall asleep. Martín and Adriana kept on talking about how they would hug their dad and not let go of him. They also mentioned that maybe Victor would not be able to recognize them, given that it had been more than a year since they last saw each other. Finally, and for Maya's sake, both kids fell asleep; one on each side of their mom. To their own surprise, the plane started descending, which meant that they could finally see North America. Glued to the tiny window, both siblings saw their first glimpse of Ontario. They even saw what seemed to be a frozen drip of water that for them was no big deal until the captain on the PA system told everyone in English and then in Spanish that they were flying above Niagara Falls. "How could that be Niagara Falls, asked a very perplexed Maya", as the falls seemed small, frozen and covered with snow. In matters of what seemed a minute, the plane had descended even more and all of the passengers on the left hand side of the plane were able to see the skyscrapers of Toronto. That view only lasted a very short time, given that the plane landed without any issues at the airport.

Everyone clapped with joy and thankfulness that they had finally made it to Canada, and so did Martín, Adriana and Maya.

Once out of the airplane, the family made it through immigration and customs with no issues. Then… the moment of truth; the one the three were waiting for. The gates opened, allowing all of the passengers from distinct flights to congregate and meet their loved ones. Martín could not have opened his eyes any wider, trying to point out his dad from a sea of people. He could not make out where his dad could be, and this was generating a bit of anxiety in his mind. He kept on looking towards his mom, thinking that maybe Victor forgot to come, or got stuck in traffic, although the streets seemed empty from up above. The thought of maybe having landed in the wrong city or airport, also made its way to his head. In fact, he ended up pronouncing it to his family. At this moment, Martín felt the wintery cold shaking his short frame, from head to toe. He started thinking about the harsh weather that he could see through the window, and the fact that his dad was not around yet, made him fixate on a negative feeling. Until he received the biggest squeeze from his blind spot, not expecting anyone there. It was Victor, who happened to have caught all three of them, setting his sight on them like a hawk flying through a moving forest. – *Hijo de mi alma* (my beloved son) –, cried out Victor, throwing his arms around Martín, as if he knew that his hug would take away the cold that Martín was starting to feel. – *Papá* –, exclaimed Martín, who was immediately joined by his mom and sister on the hug. Embracing the moment, all four stood quiet, pretending not to care for the commotion of a busy airport. If Martín had felt some type of negative feeling as he waited for his dad, by that moment, all of it vanished, allowing way for tears from all four of them, not believing the fact that they were united again. Not caring for their belongings or the time, they continued hugging each other for as long as they could, pronouncing only excitement, gratitude and relief. They exchanged a few remarks about the flight, not forgetting to mention the turmoil in the air. Nonetheless, it seemed that any bump, hiccup or negative feeling had stayed behind and by now they could only rejoice in being united to never again separate. Thank God that there were two of Victor's new friends that later became part of their family, to help transport the family to their new home. Victor and Martín rode back to their apartment with Horace and Fenny and Adriana and Maya did the same with another friend. However, before they stepped out of the airport, Victor handed the three travelers each a parka, a pair of gloves, a tuque and even a scarf. Unfortunately, he did not have enough money to buy any snow boots and therefore did not bring any to the airport. However, the walk to the car was made essentially on a fresh plowed sidewalk. Adriana and Martín did not mind at all, and thought that it was nice and funny to walk on white sidewalks and shiny asphalt.

Victor could not take his eyes off his sidekick, Martín. He could not stop giving thanks to God for him. He could also not believe how big both kids had gotten, especially Adriana, who by then was already a young lady at thirteen, whereas, Martín was taller and seemed to be more mature. Victor rode in the back with his son and would not let Horace take that spot, as he did not want to waste one second away from his son. He kept his eyes on Martín, and while caressing his head, kept on calling him "champ".

By the time they got to their new humble dwelling, Victor gave them a tour that lasted less than sixty seconds all, while the friends that helped transport the family from the airport, helped bring the luggage into the apartment. Victor and Maya did not know how to thank the generosity of their friends. Fenny and Horace, who ended up staying with the newcomers, would not take anything in return for the favour just performed. For this couple, the love evidenced by the family of four was enough payment for them. Nevertheless, after savouring a good coffee and some Tim Horton doughnuts that they also had brought to the newcomers, Fenny and Horace decided to leave, allowing the four to settle in. Victor accompanied the couple outside to their car and did not know how to thank them. Fenny, once again, reminded him that there was no need whatsoever to talk about paying anyone back, and that both she and her husband, Horace, felt that their new friendship was more than enough compensation. – How is it that I am so blessed by your friendship – inquired Victor to the couple. Fenny just looked up into the heavens and said – He who is up there shows us grace and mercy… and to him we should be thankful, always. –   Though Victor did not understand what Fenny and Horace were saying, sooner or later, he would understand the message… I'm sure of it.

– Okay, gang. We are here –, pronounced Fenny, the moment she arrived in Orillia while parking the car in a vacant lot. The two hours of driving seemed to have gone faster than expected. This solemn and pretty ride allowed Martín's parents to get to know Fenny and Horace more, while letting Adriana and Martín contemplate the beauty of nature and for the kid specifically, to reminisce with fondness, thoughts of their relatives back at home whom they still missed a lot. He had to focus now on the gains his family had achieved, like being together with daddy in a country that opened its doors for a better future. For his parent's sake, he did not want to show any disappointments or negative thoughts of being here. In fact, he appreciated and understood the family's sacrifice, led by a selfless father who forwent his career and lifestyle for his family's sake. Amidst the numerous attempts to show happiness for his new experience in Canada, there were always moments where his brain would take him back to his home (Maya out of all of them understood the issue more than anyone and would try to evoke certain heartwarming memories with the extended relatives, assuring both kids that their visit back home will come sooner than expected).

"Wow, what a view!" was essentially what all of them said the moment they got out of the car. Seeing what they would have considered a majestic view of the sea, immediately made them feel warm inside amidst the cool and fresh breeze scraping the surface of the lake and landing on their faces, making them feel awake and rejuvenated. – Thank you –, said Maya to Fenny while also giving her a hug. Fenny was happy to receive Maya's gratitude expressed in the hug but also replied to Maya while pointing up to the sky – to Him, we need to be thankful, for it is He who has given us the opportunity to enjoy life the way it is supposed to be enjoyed when we recognize His plan in our life. – Although Maya did not understand much of what Fenny was saying, she would later agree that in our journey we must become blessings to others, especially those in need. This is how we truly show our understanding of a loving the God, who gave it his all for our sake. With this idea in mind, Fenny and Horace would lead their life, seeking ways to show God's love to everyone, especially those in need. Their mission was to feed the hungry, give hope to those who felt hopeless, clothe the ones who were 'naked', among many other things. Their faith in their saviour Jesus, felt alive and contagious and it made others around them inquire more, wanting to try the sweet Good News. Soon the entire family would become enamoured with the way of life and would also seek ways to bless others, whether through an open ear, a helping hand, a ride to church or even other places, providing counselling or even showing an unselfish friendship. The few hours that the six of them spent in Orillia seemed to go faster than all of them expected. The tuna sandwiches along with the refreshments that Fenny and Horace had packed for a picnic for six was quickly consumed by six hungry and appreciative members. – It could not taste any better –, mentioned Horace which was soon after seconded by Victor while taking his last bite.

After consuming their food, all six took time to walk around the lake, visit the small picturesque town, and go in and out of the themed stores available for the tourists and locals. The last minutes of their stay in this mystique town, was spent at a lake nearby where the six would admire the presence of a beautiful and majestic sunset, making its way to the bottom of the lake. Fenny and Horace left the scene. Glancing back, they noticed a serene view. The family still remained motionless. All four of them still holding hands and in awe of the kindness, providence and unconditional love shown to their family. – What a view –, Horace mentioned to his wife, not necessarily referring to the sunset, but rather of the four in front of them. A few minutes passed by and the car was once again packed with people. Saying their goodbyes to Orillia and hopeful to return once again, in the near future.

Chapter 10 – Baseball, The Other Beautiful Game

The look down the hallway at school was what reminded Martín of the passenger boarding bridge that connected the airport's gate to the airplane. When he came out of the bathroom to go to his class, the long hallway was empty and dismal looking. All of the kids were inside their classrooms, leaving the corridor, muddy and dirty with papers that had been dropped and not picked up. He stopped for a second looking down the walkway and somehow expecting to see the side doors of the school opening up and showing the presence of his uncle Luchín. His eyes filled up once again, suddenly his teacher Mrs. Chan came out of her room not understanding why her knew student was lost in thought, but guessing that he was still struggling emotionally, she called him into her room. Clearing her throat, she interrupted Martín's contemplations and brought him back to reality. She then deduced his turmoil and interpreted it as missing his home country. – It is tough to start again in a new country and leave behind the people you love –, said Mrs. Chan with a soft and delicate voice, soothing away his pain. He understood the gist of her message, but got a clear picture when she took him towards a world map she had hanging on her bulletin board. The interesting thing about the map was that there were two pins joined together by a long yellow string. One of the pins was on Toronto, Canada and the other one was on Taipei, Taiwan. Martín followed the string from the first city all the way to the Eastern country exclaiming a "wow". She then went on explaining that when she was nineteen years of age, she left her home country to come to Canada and study at a university. Although the plan was to finish her degree and then go back home to work, she ended up staying as she met her sweetheart and got married. Without giving too much personal details, she mentioned that her parents still lived in Taiwan, very far away from her and that she still missed them. She then grabbed a picture and showed him her parents. – It is very difficult to leave people you love behind, but you will see them again –, she exclaimed. Martín understood the whole message and suddenly felt comforted by his teacher. A feeling of hope began growing in him, knowing that his teacher also missed her beloved family tremendously. Sometimes words are not needed for a teacher to be able to show and express care and belonging to a student, especially when the latter one demonstrates a need to be part of a group.

The picture started looking less gloomy and more vivid for Martín. This coming precisely around the time of the transition from winter into spring. A new beginning, filled with optimism, blooming not only roses but buds of hope. Overjoying the green grass with downpours and showers of warm sunny rays. Soon it was time to start the practices of what Martín considered "the second most beautiful game", baseball.

"How can dead trees become full of life again?", pondered Martín's family. No one could understand the process of hibernation and how buds would wake up after a long cold slumber that would make you forget that the hot summer days once existed. The days seemed longer for Martín, in fact, they were actually. The sun remained out and about for a longer period, filling everyone with joy and plans for the weekend. Kids were joining sports teams and the parks were beginning to fill up with players, parents and spectators. You could see more people outside, as if they finally decided to socialize with each other. The cold weather had made everyone stay inside, unless you needed to go shopping or to work. This brought a certain joy to Martín and his family. There was a sense of livelihood similar to the one Martín had experienced back at home.

School also became longer than expected, as every day after the last bell had rung, there was baseball practice. Everyone in the team was expected to be present and practice. This became problematic for Martín, given that his parents kept on questioning his late arrivals at home. "I have baseball practice" he would reply after being asked every time. This made his mom come one day during the practice to corroborate what her son was saying. To her surprise, she saw her son practicing with his team, and he was really talented. She did not understand how he could demonstrate and attain high skills in a sport so easily when he had not played it before. He seemed like a natural. She was very pleased to see him having fun and following instructions very well. She wished that Victor could be there watching also. Mrs. Chan passed by to see the team practice before going home, and also noticed that Martín's mom was there. She decided to sit beside her and chat. – He is really good –, pointing at Martín and affirmed his mom, who happened to understand the message quite well. – Thank you –, the mom replied. Both ladies, continued chatting about Martín, and Mrs. Chan would not stop talking about how he was starting to turn things around in school. She mentioned that he was a good kid and that he was trying very much to learn English. Mrs. Chan also mentioned how difficult it is to adjust to a culture, a new way of living, and to the crude winter; elements that had a tremendous impact on newcomers. She really understood her student, maybe due to the fact that she had also once experienced the same struggles, and walked through the same rocky road. One thing was for sure, she had the right touch to make any anxious heart become soothed and calm. A characteristic that she held dearly and knew how to use in blessing others. Even Maya felt this way while speaking to her.

The practice lasted a little longer than an hour. All of the kids helped the coach bring the equipment back to the gym. Once they finished they were all dismissed. Martín went to his mom and was very surprised to see her there speaking to his favourite teacher. After giving her a hug, they both started making their way back home.

Their walk was nothing but exciting, given that Martín talked the entire way back. He informed his mom of the play by play that took place during the practice. His excitement was over the roof and his mom could not be any happier for him. She started noticing that her son was having a better time at school. The fact that he was stoked made her feel happy, and even more so, after speaking to a caring and patient teacher, Mrs. Chan. His excitement was so contagious that she wanted to share the happenings with her husband. And that was exactly what she did, the moment Victor opened the door to let them in. She talked about Martín and how good he was at playing baseball.

– Isn't there any soccer? –, asked Victor.

– No, dad. In Canada, we play baseball not soccer. I need to play baseball with my friends –, answered Martín as if trying to convince his dad. Maya looked at her husband trying to let him know to celebrate his son's accomplishments rather than question them. He got the point and immediately patted Martín's back saying – good job, son. I am so proud of you. When is your game? I would love to be there –, he asserted.

– Dad, the coach said that I am really good and that he wants me to play for an after-school league. Do you think I can join? – asked a very excited young boy.

– Son, how much is it going to cost? Remember that we are very tight with money right now, and I am still paying off the expenses to Canada. –

Although his dad did not want to extinguish Martín's dream of playing ball by bringing up the finances, he did. Martín also understood that he should not be asking for anything that may cost money, due to the family's circumstances, and decided to change the topic and discuss the friends that he was making at school. The mom picked upon the issue right away, and staying quiet from her seat, she thought of a way to make the money available for his son's new sport. Her attempts of getting a job were in vain, given her little to no English language skills. In addition to this, the amount of money that her husband was making was merely enough for the rent, his transportation to work and the food placed on the table.

Although Martín recognized not to ask for anything that required money, and although he was not okay about it, he knew that he had to show a higher level of maturity, and therefore tried to understand. Unfortunately, he thought that the best thing to do was to focus only on the baseball practices and forget about playing in a summer league. His embarrassment regarding the family's financial deficiency was something that blocked him from participating in numerous school activities. When asked to partake on school trips, he would simply say that he was not allowed, and quickly toss away the permission note. In fact, he would never bring any of them to his parents. It seemed like the conversation he had with his dad regarding the summer league, marked him deeply that he applied his dad's thinking to any expenditure. Good thing that the teacher never asked questions regarding the lack of participation in the trips, which made it easier for Martín, as he did not have to explain anything. He would just stay in school with his favourite teacher, Mrs. Chan.

The baseball tournament came sooner than expected. All of the kids in the team were elated, and it was not different for Martín, who had finally felt part of a team. For the past two weeks, he had been practicing almost every day after school with the other kids. There were instances where he would even practice on his own or with his dad, once he came home from work. Both he and his dad looked forward to going to the park and playing some catch, or even bat a few pop flies and grounders. Even Adriana would come to the park and fetch some of the balls back to the two boys. They enjoyed their time in the park so much that kids in the area would watch and ask to join in. There was also Mo who happened to attend the same park on that precise day. Martín continued feeling very anxious around him and quickly decided to walk closer to his dad, as if he were using him to hide without saying anything. His dad noticed that there was something not right in his reaction, but was not sure what exactly. He also saw a young boy, about his own son's age approaching them and watching from a distance. Mo happened to like seeing Martín with his dad and sister playing ball and wanted to join in, but did not ask. However, Victor noticed his eagerness to participate in the play and asked him – hey, you want play? – –*papá*, no *por favor*–, exclaimed an uneasy Martín, begging his dad not to ask that boy. –

Son, I don't know why you don't want him to join, but if there is something wrong with this kid, avoiding him or being mean to him will not help the situation –. Martín understood what his dad said, yet decided to not step too far away from his dad. Mo shook Victor's hand, greeted his peer and waved at Adriana. He also said his name to everyone and joined the game. He then told Martín to separate on two sides so that they could cover more area. Martín understood the message and liked the idea. Though he still felt bad for the situation that Mo experienced with his dad, he still did not trust him to become his friend, especially after being bullied by him since day one. Good thing that kids tend not to hold onto grudges as easily as adults do, and in a matter of a short period both kids were having a fantastic time playing ball with Adriana and Victor.

It seemed as if the two hours that had just passed by turned into thirty minutes, and that was because nobody thought about how late it was becoming due to the longer days. The sun was setting a bit later than what Martín had seen, and this meant that the family needed to go back home. As he started grabbing all of his belongings, Mo approached him with a helping hand and said to his new friend – thank you for letting me play with you guys and sorry for being mean to you. – The message could not be any clearer for Martín, and for this reason his jaw dropped and his eyes communicated shock, showing his big dark eyes. – Ok, see you tomorrow –, he replied, shaking his hand. – See son, what did I tell you? The best way to pay evil is with good. Now you have made a friend by showing him mercy and not punishment –, exclaimed Victor to a very happy yet still surprised son. – *Gracias, papa* –, he mentioned while giving him an enormous squeeze. His dad kissed him on the head, looked up and pronounced a voiceless – thank you –. He still could not believe that he was in Canada and united with his own family.

The tournament came sooner than expected and unfortunately for Victor, he could not attend it due to work. The good thing was that both Maya and Adriana did show up to cheer for their beloved Martín. In fact, Fenny also came with a camcorder used to record the game. Victor was so happy that at least he had the video to watch over and over again. The day was filled with high and lows, much exercise and joy. Martín's team did very well. As a matter of fact, they made it all the way to the finals. This was the first time that Martín had been part of a team, and the excitement that he was feeling at that moment was definitely very similar to the one he felt during his karate tournament. The biggest downfall was that his uncle Luchín, known as his "partner in crime", was not there to watch, which was still difficult for Martín to swallow. Good thing that Maya's intuition as a mother, allowed her to decipher the temporary sadness that hid behind his eyes, and then reminded him that his uncle would be so proud of him.

– Let's play ball–, shouted the umpire, and quickly both teams moved to their appropriate spots. Martín's team was the first to bat and it was precisely he who was told by the coach to bat first. The first pitch came and he did not move, – Strike one –, screamed the umpire. – Focus, son–, yelled the coach from the dugout. He quickly looked at his coach and nodded his head. The second pitch came and as fast as it came, it left. Given that the impact from the lumber made the trajectory of the ball go far as it could go, allowing the batter to land in third. – A perfect hit – shouted the coach, showing a smile from ear to ear. Unfortunately for him that satisfaction disappeared faster than the hit, since the next three hitters either struck out or popped out. Luckily the other team's three batters also struck out in sequence, not posing any type of threat. The game was only five innings and the first four seemed to be a clear and perfect repetition of the first one. However, on the last inning with already two outs, Martín stepped up to the plate. This time he did not wait for the two pitches to swing, and took a crack on the first one, making the outfielders fetch for the ball. Martín ran the bases as fast as possible, galloping his way to home base and scoring the first and only run of the game. This permitted the team to win the game and advance to the next round.

The boys from the team became relaxed and were not nervous anymore. It seemed like their family's presence helped everyone there. During their downtime, while it was the time for other teams to play, the coach reminded them to eat light and often, to hydrate and to continue moving and practice catching and hitting. Certainly, this helped the team remain poised and focused for the following two other games. The final game was the most exciting one, however, if you were to ask the coach or any of the players on Martín's team, they would say that it was wild and heart attack worthy. Due to the fact that the opponent started off with a five–straight run inning, whereas their team had a straight three up, three down for the first four innings, this caused immense anticipation for both the team and audience. By the fifth and final inning the team was down by as many as half a dozen and quite honestly, it seemed like everyone had already lost hope of a championship banner being raised in their gym. With no one out, it was Mo's turn to bat. He squared himself into position and waited for the first pitch. – Ball –, yelled the umpire. Mo moved away from his stance and removed the dirt off his cleats by hitting them with the bat. He quickly readjusted his gloves and helmet and got ready once again. The pitch was just like the first one, low and fast. Mo swung his bat like a golf club and made contact with the ball, which went up in the sky and away from the diamond. It was gone! A solo homerun to put the team on the scoreboard. Some of his team cheered him and greeted Mo back in the dugout but the majority of the team had the attitude of – too little, too late –. The next two batters were somehow able to make it to a base by hitting grounders. The following batter struck out, however, the next batter cleared the bases and landed on second base. The score was now six to three with only one out. Martín's turn came up and he also hit a good pitch, allowing him to bring another runner home as he landed on second base. It was six to four. The next player popped out, but his hit was deep enough to force a steal to third. Now with two outs and two runs behind, Richard came to bat and as the ball met the bat, his majestic swing made the ball pretty much disappear from the field, tying the game at six a piece. No one could believe it, not even the coach. With one out left, the team still had hopes of winning the game. The next three hitters all got singles and with the bases loaded the next batter cleared them, making the second triple of the game. Now Martín's team was on top by three runs, and that was how the top of the inning ended. The bottom of the inning was such a sweet surprise. There was one strike out but the next two plays came from feline-like kids. The first one made the defender extend his arm as far as possible to catch a pop fly, whereas the final out came right after the opponent had scored two runs from solo homeruns to creep up their score to under one. The coach called for a time out and all of the players from the infield came together to talk. The advice was sweet and to the point. – Keep your eye on the ball, pitch away from the batter, and cover your area well –. The next hitter made contact with the ball. The sound of cracking wood like the one made from a log in a bonfire was even heard from every corner from the bleachers. The hit was good, looping the ball into a green patch of unprotected sod, yet out of nowhere came flying Martín, making an over his shoulder diving catch. He extended his arm out to show the ball, as the rest of the team came out running towards him and diving either beside him or on top of him, creating a human pyramid of cheerful kids. The parents watching got up and cheered for both teams for their fantastic performance. The opposite team could not believe how they had lost the game, and their coach thought that he was pickpocketed in such a subtle way. However, he recognized the heart and soul of both teams. He was the first person to congratulate the winning team. Stopping at Martín and kneeling down to his level he said – You are really good, kid. Don't let anyone ever put you down. – It seemed like this coach knew the struggles that overtook Martín the first few months at school. He glanced back at the coach and replied with a gentle "thank you", and a smile that showed his great satisfaction.

Martín could not wait to tell his dad how he was chosen as the MVP of the tournament and of his own team. He was so proud and felt like finally he belonged in his new school. That sense of excitement was carried to the school, home, church and everywhere he would go. That is, because he decided to wear both his MVP pins on his t-shirt, showing off what he would call, his greatest achievement. His parents were happier to a greater extent than he was. In fact, Victor ended up taking both the pins and showing them off at his work the next day. For the parents, any of the kid's accomplishments automatically became theirs. Maya, although also thrilled for her son's new triumph, was pleased that he was finally fitting in.

You may ask about that boy Mo, and what happened between he and Martín. Well, a friendship did sprout, but not immediately, which would have been the way that Martín or anyone would have liked, but at least for the time remaining in school, Mo did not taunt him again. In fact, during recess time, when the kids would gather to play baseball, the participants would divide into two teams, with Mo being the captain of one and Martín being chosen by Mo. "Better to be closer to him, than against him ", thought Martín, and this made him content, to think that he had no more enemies anymore. However, the living hell that Mo still carried in his life, was enough to describe his behavior as a ticking time bomb.

Chapter 11 – The Story of Mo

His name was Moses (although everyone at school knew him by "Mo") and he too, was born into a family of immigrants. His own dad, named Isak, came to Canada when he was a teenager, about nineteen, fleeing religious persecution from a war-torn country. The instability of the new government leader made it difficult for many of the country's citizens to enjoy a peaceful life. Isak had sadly witnessed the death of his own parents, outside of their home, by the paramilitary agents who had come to try to convert everyone in the village. "Faith or death" was their slogan. Some people chose the first one, renouncing their own belief system, in order to keep their children and family members out of danger. Others were not as fortunate, and chose their own way of living, which sadly cost them their lives. Isak was also attacked by this army, and to his dismay, he was left unconscious, lying in his own pool of blood that was pouring out from his injured leg. – Leave him behind –, mentioned one of the officers to his comrade, after his mate had run out of bullets. – If he is not dead, he will die soon –. The paramilitary officers left the village after having burned down houses and leaving many bodies behind. Isak was one of the few who had remained alive, but was not tended to after until a group of volunteers from the USA/Canada had come to intervene and take care of the horrific aftermath. Quickly they noticed that Isak was alive, but his vitals were weak and in much need of urgent medical intervention. Half a dozen of the volunteers came over to treat him. It was as if they had won the lottery by finding a heartbeat still pumping, given that their enthusiasm was over the roof. Many would have said that Isak was a lost cause, even he would have told you that it would have been better to leave him for dead. But not this group of courageous and generous people, whose only mission was to serve.

Isak was taken to a nearby hospital and soon after had surgery on his leg. Although his body craved blood from the loss earlier that day, somehow it seemed like he was still hanging on by a fine thin thread. The group of men and women that had come to his salvation stayed behind, expecting to see this poor guy recovered. They were all that he had now, after the loss of both his parents. Following a period of a few hours of an intense procedure, the doctor came out to advise the group that the patient was out of danger. They all hugged each other, demonstrating their complete satisfaction for the preserving of a life. – Can one of us go see him –, asked the older person from the group. – Maybe not now, as the patient needs to rest –, replied the doctor, – but hopefully by tomorrow you can go in and see him –. The group of people thanked the doctor for his arduous work and one by one left the hospital waiting room. They knew that their volunteer assignment was shaping up to be a calling of life.

The next day the same group of five individuals came back to the hospital. Each of them very thankful after finding out that their new friend was awake. Unfortunately for them, Isak's spirit was low and in a very dark place, after recalling that his parents were executed in front of him. Chris, who was the oldest out of the group, was chosen to be the one to enter the hospital room and meet Isak. He knew that the task of seeing the wounded was going to be a difficult one, but what he never imagined was next:

– Good morning, Isak. My name is Chris. –

– Yes, I know who you are -, replied Isak with a very negative demeanor. This took Chris for a surprise, as he was not expecting this type of an answer.

– I am sorry, Isak but we wanted to introduce ourselves and let you know that if you need anything that we are here to help you. –

– Can you answer a question –, asked Isak to Chris who by now felt like he was walking on eggshells.

– Yes, anything –, replied Chris

– Why didn't you and your group let me die? What business do I have now to live in this misery? –

– Isak, I am so sorry for the loss of your parents. Although I do not know how this may feel, let me assure you that I on behalf of our group… –

– Yes, you cannot imagine how this feels. You will never be able to fathom the idea of seeing your parents being murdered in front of your own eyes. What is life now but a hollow bag of unending sorrows. I don't want to continue living. What am I going to do once I get out? Are you going to take care of me? I don't think so. –

There was a long pause and Chris knew that anything that he could say, would not make Isak feel any better. The damage was done. The losses were real, yet the help was authentic.

– You are right, Isak… I won't know how this may feel, and I won't pretend to either. Please know that our intentions are to help you out. We do not have a hidden agenda… We're here only if you allow us to be, and we promise you that we'll not leave you. –Chris replied earnestly.

Isak did not know what this help entailed and was still too hurt to actually realize the magnitude of Chris and his group's support. However, with time he found out the selfless act of kindness that reigned in the hearts of Chris and his crew. Soon Isak was able to leave the hospital's urgent care unit and be transferred to a centre where he would have full time care, while recuperating from his wounds. Although the process was long and at times it felt lonely, Isak did recover fully; at least physically. He ended up working in the same centre that took care of him, while waiting for his application to Canada. He also tended to others with similar stories. This is where he met his girlfriend, Marja, the mother of Mo. Their love story quickly grew and it seemed as if Isak had a new meaning to life. She also had been a victim of the same sorrows that took away Isak's parents. She too had significant loses that she suffered a few years ago, but her vantage to life was one filled with hope. Her determination to seek life's little pleasure of happiness was not overshadowed by her current familial situation. She was a strong woman, feisty and willing to fight any battle, even if loss was the only result. Isak would have never known this, and that is because she never shared it with anyone, but the day the paramilitary officers came to her house and took literally everything she owned, she fought one of the officers, striking him more than once in the head, although not causing any meaningful harm towards him. She on the other side, suffered much loss and was left thrown on the floor after being slapped across the face. This time, the officers did not do anything else against her and left her in her miseries, deposed of pretty much everything she owned in her little palace-like home. Her losses were boundless, nonetheless, she could not be any more content to be alive and with good health. She did not fixate on what she just lost, but rather on the fact that she still had her health intact and a hunger to surpass all obstacles in life. This sense of empowerment mixed with optimism, attracted Isak to her, and somehow felt complete and with confidence. His happiness was notorious and at times, contagious. "It was finally good to have him around" many felt and would comment.

Their love grew to the commencement of a new seed in her, but rapidly became tainted the moment they found out that her terminal cancer was also growing within. It was either the baby or her, but not both. He knew in his heart that the treatment she needed was more important than the fruit of their love. – You can get pregnant again –, Isak supplicated her. He truly felt that her health was more important not only for her but for his life too. She did not see eye to eye with him and felt that what she carried joyously, would be the culminating act of their love. She could not allow this "product of their love" to be extinguished. She wanted to keep the baby and give birth to new life, though fully knowing that this would pose a high risk to her life, given that the inability of starting any type of treatment during a pregnancy, would signify a considerable growth, leading to her own death.

The months passed by rapidly and the moment came where their baby, Mo made his debut into this world. His birth was also very fast, which was a blessing for Marja who was weak and soon-to-exit. Miraculously, holding her newborn by her bosom gave her courage and peace for a few seconds. Time stopped. So it seemed, for this new mother. She hugged him and kissed his tiny forehead. There is no stronger love than that of a mother towards her baby. The doctors witnessed a true act of love, while Isak hoped to perceive a healing miracle for his sake and also for the soon-to-be baby orphan. Tragically, the entry of the newborn also meant her exit. She called for Isak, kissed him with the little amount of energy left on her, gave him the baby and pronounced – this is my gift to you –. Soon after that, she closed her eyes once more, never to open them again. Isak felt overwhelmed and the commotion from within overtook him, bringing him down to his knees in front of the woman that he loved and making him cry like an inconsolable baby.

His life was not the same anymore. That glimpse of happiness that represented his better half, immediately escaped his eyes, bringing him back to his ruins. He could not take care of a newborn and quite honestly did not even have the strength nor desire to do so. Little Mo reminded him of the love he has for his wife. At times, he would drown his sorrows in fermented barley, temporarily forgetting his past, not wanting to think of the present nor plan for the future. If it wasn't for Chris, who made it his mission to visit him often and become a big brother, Isak would not have had the chance to continue forward. In fact, Chris became the unofficial uncle of Mo and at times, the only father figure. Chris and his mission group worked tirelessly into bringing Isak and Mo to Canada in order to start fresh. A young, single father with clear physical injuries, needed all the support he could get, although his pride, immaturity and lack of knowledge would impede him from even asking for a helping hand.

A year after her death, Isak found out some news that would allow him and his son to come to Canada. However, it was notorious that Chris was happier than Isak about this. – This is my hometown and you are going to love it there –, mentioned a very excited Chris to a not-so-thrilled Isak. It was very obvious that the latter was drowning in his sorrows, hindering any speck of joy from growing. He was nineteen but had endured certain situations that even a retired person would have never undergone. Now with a new light shining in the horizon, he took his baby, packed his few possessions and listened to Chris' advice and landed in Canada, where he would meet more individuals like Chris. Unfortunately for Mo, Isak submerged himself in his addiction to alcohol. He became dependent on the bottle and almost lost Mo when the kid was just a toddler. Isak became the only father figure for Mo, nonetheless, he found this title was too big of a responsibility to be carried over his shoulders. As a matter of fact, Isak was more absent (although he was always at home watching television and drinking beer) than involved in the life of Mo. Now, being eleven years old, Mo had little to no respect towards his dad and for the most part a lack of respect towards any authority. The lack of a mother and the absence of a nurturing father but rather one with an authoritative and harsh persona, led Mo to become hostile, disoriented in his education, and a disrespectful attitude towards others. In fact, the episode that Martín witnessed just outside Mo's house would be one that would repeat itself over and over, making Mo sleep at a friend's house and disappear momentarily. Isak did not show any feelings of a caring parent. As long as he could collect his childcare benefit (a monthly check that would make its way to all parents with kids under eighteen years of age) and buy more beer, he would be content. Mo, on the other hand, could not wait to turn sixteen, so that he could abandon the place he often referred to as a "hell-hole".

Maybe you would understand why Mo was so harsh to Martín based on his family experience. It only takes an absent parent to create enough anger in one child, to feel unloved and not understood, or to become aggressive towards others. In addition, he was never remorseful and showed a constant apathetic trait towards others. Mo felt like the world had given him two left feet for the final gala. His way to express his complete dissatisfaction towards others was to bully those he considered weak. Good thing for him that his homeroom teacher had extra time for him, and would allow Mo to stay behind after class to help put away some of the class resources that the kids had used during instruction time. Mo, enjoyed staying behind, embracing the fact that there was someone who cared enough for him. The importance of a caring adult who invested a bit of extra time allowed the boy to feel valuable and wanted. Unfortunately, every day after school, Mo would have to go back home and witness the life of an adult that he considered pitiful and had no respect for. At times, Mo would have to make himself a simple sandwich with some cut up veggies that were found in a corner of an empty refrigerator, next to a greenish looking cup of yogurt that never got eaten.

After reflecting on Mo's dire situation, it triggered a memory Martín had about his first day of school. It started at the main office with both parents being present with a family friend who acted as the interpreter. His parents were excited that Martín was going to be starting school. Mo ended up bringing the attendance down to the office and saw Martín's dad giving him a big hug and a goodbye kiss on the forehead. Seeing how loving the dad was, made Mo very upset and jealous, reminding him of the lack of affection he had in his own life. This is why Mo showed so much hatred towards Martín without necessarily knowing that he disliked him. However, by now (soon after the baseball tournament), Mo had started to show a glimpse of contentment towards Martín. Maya had also recognized that there was some type of issue between the two boys and when she had the opportunity to be kind to him, she was. During the tournament, she tried very hard to communicate with him, using her little amount of English, mixed with her vast knowledge in child psychology and motherly intuition. This all allowed her to eventually realize that he was the reason why her own son did not want to go to school. She handed Mo a peeled orange, which he took without hesitation. Then she gave him one of Martín's juice boxes and said – drink –. Once again, he did not refute and gladly took it. Although he did not say a – thank you – the smile he demonstrated was enough to be understood as great satisfaction. That was another victory, and one that Maya considered a great one; the fact that she could interact in a positive way with the boy that was antagonizing her own son. Some mothers and even dads would have probably been upset and would have shown a sense of dislike towards the aggressor. However, Maya knew as a professional and as a mother, that this technique would only have a snowball effect on her own son, but while showing compassion through her charismatic and nurturing way, would help establish a deeper connection.

Maybe this is why Mo disliked Martín. Perhaps because Martín had a mother and a father who cared for him, and loved him. And if you thought like this, you were probably very right. Maya, having volunteered at the school for a few days had already confirmed her maternal instincts by sensing harm against her son from Mo. Therefore, every day that she volunteered at school, she would make sure to serve the milk to Martín's class. In fact, when all of the students lined up to receive their ration, she made sure to give a bit extra to Mo, who usually accepted this with open arms. She knew that the boy lacked food, and not because she had seen his lunches, but because his skinny figure and shorter stature for an eleven-year-old boy was pronounced. She also knew how it was to live with little to almost nothing, given that a few months ago she had undergone a tough situation in her own country, lacking many of the essentials. Not to say that now in Canada she had plenty, but at least the family was together, and as little as her husband made, it was enough to be efficiently used for groceries and rent money.

What really surprised Martín was that one day after school, Maya came to pick up Martín from school, and while walking home, they both witnessed a similar situation between Mo and his father, confirming to Maya the familial deficiency that that poor boy was having. She did not see as much as what Martín had witnessed more than a month ago, but it was enough to conclude as that what Mo was going through was simply abuse. Maya and Martín did not hide behind a bush, like Martín once did, instead she called Mo, who happened to be distraught and mad, but the moment he saw Maya, he ran to her and hugged her, making Martín feel jealous for a split second. He then understood that Mo did not have a mother and needed the support of one in order to function properly as a child. To be honest, he did not come to this conclusion on his own, but rather because his mom had mentioned it to him several times while trying to explain why poor Mo needed compassion from Martín. – Me... be nice to him? But he has been the one who has hurt me several times. How can I be nice to someone who belittles me? –. Maya understood her son's queries but was not willing to budge on paying good to all, even if they harm you. So, to Martín's surprise, he had to bring a double lunch the next day and hand one over to Mo, with a smile. However, up to this point, Mo was already trying to change his conduct towards his used-to-be-known "nemesis". – Thank you – was what he said the next day after receiving a brown bag that looked like the other one that Martín had. – Do you want to eat together? – asked a grateful young boy. Martín was not sure what had happened, and although he was already living a school-life free of Mo's shenanigans, this still did not mean that he saw him as a good kid. Nonetheless, that last month of school was one that Martín would remember as one of his best. He and Mo became closer friends and it seem like the positive impact that one was making on the other was real and very effective, though it did not help when going back home with his dad. Nevertheless, Mo knew that he would never run out of milk to drink at school, or a lunch that was shared with him by his now new friend, Martín. A confidante was just what Martín missed the most from his hometown, Lima, and was searching for one now in his new country. Nevertheless, Martín would unconsciously evoke his wonderful times with his Peruvian *amigo*.

Chapter 12 – Martín's Best Friend in Peru

– Hi, my name is Waldo. Do you want to play chess? – inquired a young a nine-year-old boy who back in Peru, lived in the same apartment building Martín's dad had recently purchased one a year before his odyssey to North America. Martín did not know what to think, since he had not played this game with a young person before. Although he had very little understanding of the game and had played with his dad in the past, he believed he had enough skills to show off to this new kid. Waldo quickly made room on a rustic half stained bench and set up his game. As they were playing, Martín was a bit surprised to find out that he was winning so easily and that Waldo was losing every single piece. This just allowed Martín to become filled with confidence, trusting very much in his every move, and thinking of himself as a world-renowned chess master. The game ended just after a few minutes with an overwhelming victory from Martín. – Oh man, I can't believe how good you are. You have definitely, played this game –, replied a heavy-hearted Waldo. – Wanna play again? –, asked once again Waldo with intrigue. Martín did not think before responding and quickly said – sure – let's do it. – Wait, do you want to bet on a chocolate from the corner store? The loser can buy the winner one. What do you think? – added Waldo. – This sounds like a good plan –, responded Martín. Both boys set up the game once again and Waldo allowed Martín to choose his side. After they decided who was who, the game started, just like the first one, but with one significant difference, and one that only lasted a few seconds. For the first time ever Martín was introduced to the "Fool's Mate" move, which made him feel precisely like one, a fool! Martín looked up, away from the chess board and observed his new friend, who had a radiant smile that showed his glowing white choppers. Not saying anything, yet expecting his prize, Waldo gathered all of the pieces and placed them in its box, while Martín was still stupefied, not being able to say anything. As a matter of fact, he had nothing to say, nor could he think of anything but how much of a chump he'd been for falling prey to a shark. He quickly snapped out of his daze and looking into his pocket he found two coins that would buy him enough for two chocolates. – Don't worry, my friend –, mentioned Waldo. – Today you buy, but tomorrow I will buy –, finished saying. And this was actually very true, as Waldo would make sure to always buy all of the junk food eaten by both kids.

These two became inseparable very quickly, and Martín learned so much from his new "street smart" pal. It felt like he was learning from him every day, yet he did not mind being the kid's disciple. Good thing for his parents that his new buddy had a good heart, even though he was also known as a clown, quick witted and even charming. Soon these two were spending so much time together. Martín became Waldo's sidekick, and they both complimented each other nicely. Sometimes when the boys wanted to do something together, but Martín did not have permission to go outside for various reasons such as: cleaning his room, or eating his food or fighting with his sister, it would take Waldo a quick second to convince Martín's family that going out to play with him would be beneficial for everyone, not just for Martín. – If you allow him to come outside, I will make sure that he thinks plenty of his actions and of the importance of being well behaved. I promise you that by allowing him to go outside and play, his brain will oxygenate, helping him to think better and subsequently, to act better. You guys would have a break from him and I will try my very best to take care of him –, ended Waldo. Martín's mom and dad would finally allow Martín to go out, but not because of Waldo's "effective speech", but rather because either he was so consistent and would never give up, or because Maya thought that he was very charming and with a kind heart. Regardless of the reason, Waldo would simply be happy that his soon to be "*compadre*" was out of "prison".

These two kids became very close and hung out together every day. Soon they accompanied each other to doctor appointments, music lessons or any other extra-curricular activity the other had. Each set of parents started planning for not only their own kids, but adding one, even when going on family outings. Waldo was like a son to Maya Victor, and Martín a son to Waldo's parents.

During the summer days Waldo would sometimes accompany his dad to his workplace and have lunch usually at a place that the youngster chose. For Waldo, it was fun visiting and spending time in the back of the warehouse/store his dad managed. He knew everyone that worked there, and all of the employees treated him with respect and endearment. They called him "the mini boss" and Waldo thought that that was a funny name for him. He was very pleasant with all of them, often bringing them a gaseous refreshment or a lemonade from his dad's mini bar (this cold appliance held about thirty bottles of all types of pops and juices and even milk, both chocolate and white). For any ten-year old around, this would be the best refrigerator ever, even for Waldo and Martín. His dad did not mind and thought that what his son did with the others was very honorable and kind of him. This is why none of the employees minded having him around in their work area, chatting and often even reading quietly. The warehouse had mountains of clothes and fabrics that later would be sold to the clients and to other stores. Waldo would hang out there, in the warehouse where all of the linens were stored before being shipped. He would climb a big hill of extra pieces of linens and just sit there while reading a comic book or a kid's magazine (usually the kind that had BMX or even extreme sports). Sometimes one of the employees would bring him a drink or a snack to Waldo, so that he could continue reading quietly. Now with his new "bestie" there was no doubt for him that Martín would accompany him and his dad too. The first time Martín accompanied Waldo to the warehouse, he could not believe that Waldo's dad had a fridge filled only with pop and juices of every kind. For any kid, this was essentially a dream come true, however, Waldo's dad, although he would share a drink with the boys, would limit the amount of sugar intake for both of them. There was also a surprise that both kids really enjoyed, in which one of the employee's, having knowledge of the arrival of both kids, would have brought over to the warehouse a platter filled with treats and sugary puffy goodies that would be enjoyed by both comrades until the platter was empty.

The afternoon was well spent. Having drunk and eaten sugary delights in the morning, they had also spent the remainder of their time, making trenches with the big containers. In addition, they used boards that had wheels (for easier transportation of the linens to the truck) on the bottom, and using them as skateboards, they would glide from one end of the warehouse to the other. The employees would enjoy having young blood full of energy, (and sugar) visiting and adding a sense of jovial excitement to an already busy and at times, stressful environment. If you were to ask the employees about their feelings towards the kids in the warehouse, they would tell you that it was well received, especially because Waldo's dad would become more human and less of a "dictatorial boss" who used micromanagement as his main tool. Nevertheless, the productivity did not diminish with the visit of the kids, rather it did not even change one bit. Maybe because the kids added enjoyment to their already busy and stressful job, and this allowed them to be productive while also acquiring serenity. Unfortunately for the workers, the boys would only spend the morning at the warehouse because Waldo's dad would take both of them to a restaurant of their choice to eat. To his astonishment, the boy ordered enough food for five, and ate it all. Again, the dad could not believe that such small bodies would consume so much, as if they had not eaten all day. By the time both kids got home, they separated momentarily, going to their own homes to rest and recharge. This day was just a glimpse of how the summer season would be spent.

Another summer event that is worth mentioning is the time that both boys spent at a local television station, and being on live TV without even planning this. How did this happen? You could only imagine. That day, both kids were biking in the neighbourhood and happened to see a sign for their favourite show on a van's back window. Its message was an open invitation to all kids to come to a famous rock show with a national renowned kid's hero, and sing along on stage with him. Having memorized all of the songs, both kids could not think of a reason for not biking to the venue and appearing with their idol on the most popular kids show. Although it was Waldo who had the idea of convincing the other one to execute the plan, Martín was the one who said –it's only a few kilometers away, and with our bikes, we can be there in no time. – – But what are we going to do when they ask us for our parents? – questioned Waldo. – No worries, I will take care of it–, quickly and almost as natural as possible replied a very savvy Martín. Next thing you knew, both kids set their bikes on gear and took off to meet their destiny. Having no permission from their parents and running out of time to bike, they took the plunge and thought that becoming famous was more important than being obedient, well, at least for the time being.

The line was full of kids their age. All of them were accompanied by a parent, or at least by an adult or some sort of adult supervision. There seemed to be no child alone or quiet in line. All of them were talkative, and their excitement was quite visible. Once the big door opened, letting the kids get inside, Martín told Waldo that this was their opportunity to come in. Unfortunately for these two, one of the coordinators realized that neither boy had a name tag, just like the other kids –Stop– she exclaimed. – What seems to be the problem? – inquired a perplexed and bothered Waldo, showing a sign of annoyance for being stopped. –Where's your nametag? –, asked a lady that by now did not seem to be as empowered as when she initially stopped the two. – The man at the entrance did not give it to us because he ran out of them. Sorry but we are not going to miss our chance of being on stage with our favourite singer because of a lack of nametags. My parents will be very upset if they don't see us out there. Would you like my dad to come here? He is the right hand of the boss of the channel –, uttered a very convincing ten-year-old boy. – No... it's ok, kids. Just make sure to sign out before you leave. This way we know that your parents have picked you up –, replied the coordinator not trying to risk the kid from complaining to her superior. Both boys ran behind the other kids and quickly found themselves on stage with their childhood hero singing songs that they knew by heart. It was a dream come true for both kids. Being essentially at arm's reach with their main celebrity, singing his songs was bigger than life. The best part was when the camera man pointed his lens towards Waldo and Martín, showing the entire nation all of the lucky participants. Might as well enjoy their twenty minutes of fame, especially when at home, Adriana, was watching the same show in the comfort of her living room. Having the eyesight of an eagle, she suddenly captured the presence of both her little brother and his friend to the right side of the rocker. Quickly she pressed record on the VCR, making sure to seize the moment, specifically with Martín. She could not believe how these two boys had made it there, especially without their parents' permission. "Mom is going to have a cow", Adriana thought, while laughing quietly and recording on tape her brother's future sentence. She could only think of how to reveal the news to her parents and when would be the best time to do it. As a big sister however, she thought of the well-being of her brother and wanted to make sure that he got home safely. She decided to go down to the third floor and knock on the apartment door of Waldo, so that she could ask his parents if they knew of the whereabouts of their child. After asking for the boy and her brother, the mom replied that they both where outside biking in the neighbourhood. This is when she decided to let the oblivious lady know where her child was. Rehearsing a story about how she was viewing this show with a rock star at the most legendary TV station, she added that the boys had somehow biked their way to fame, without their parent's permission. Wilma, the mother of Waldo could not believe that her little angel could be able make his way to the show, especially without having permission. Adriana, being very precautious, had brought the tape, anticipating a disbelief from the mom. After being granted permission to show the tape to Wilma, Adriana set up the television and displayed the recording, pausing at the right moment and pointing out both her brother and Waldo. Fortunately for the boys, Wilma could not make out anything, as she was not wearing her glasses. She had accidentally left them at work that same day and was only back home for the lunch hour. However, she decided to believe Adriana, and accompanied her to her own apartment (to talk to her parents about this event who just happened to come in from their grocery shopping). When she arrived, to her surprise, was greeted by both boys, who had sped up, biking back home in record time to make it and pretended as if nothing had happened. Wilma was confused and perplexed, not knowing what to believe anymore, so she asked her son where he was. He answered, – biking outside with Martín, as we usually do –. Adriana could not believe that her brother and Waldo were back, and about to get away with their shenanigans. "How could this be?" she starting thinking but their arrival confused her and she started to doubt herself. She accidentally dropped the tape that she was holding with dear life, breaking it into two pieces, essentially burying away any circumstantial evidence she had. Now she did not know what to think anymore. Martín and Waldo, on the other hand could not stop from smiling, while at the same time gasping for air, as a result of their cycling odyssey.

These were the moments that Martín remembered and held close to his heart. Not pretending to stop the few tears that still made their way down his face every time he remembered his buddy, he would just long to have that kind of a friendship with someone else. Faced however, with the uncertainty due to the move to North America and leaving behind his relatives and friends, made him feel the lack of friendships he had at his age, and although his sister became his best bud, he still missed terribly his *compadre*. – Can I play with you –, asked Mo to a lost soul Martín who was hanging out in the neighborhood park with his sister and dad. By this time, Martín had enough social English skills to understand what Mo was asking, however, his emotions were mixed with sadness and anger towards the boy. He felt the grief that Mo was undergoing with his situation, but at the same time, he also recalled the times that this same kid was ill mannered towards him. Yet, it was the sad feeling that won his thoughts and emotions, which allowed him to answer with a simple – yes –, followed by – me dad and me sister play baseball. You can playing too. – The sentence was not properly constructed due to the lack of English skills, yet the message was clear and to the point. Victor noticed that his son had met his nemesis but someway understood that the negative relationship that these two preteens had was about to turn into something fruitful. A few laughs were manifested, accompanied by several great and memorable moments that would remind Martín of his fabulous times in Peru with his pal.

The sun began to set behind the horizon, reminding everyone that it was a school night, and the time to go inside and get ready for bed was imminent. Martín grabbed the little baseball equipment he owned and said to Mo – see you –. Then went on to his dad and sister to start their walk to the house. Nevertheless, Victor noticed that Mo was not getting ready to go to his house and was pretending to stay longer in the park, making his way to the play structure. The concerned parent asked his own son about Mo's situation, and Martín quickly replied that his peer would stay in the park until way after the sunset. Victor did not like this but at the same time did not know how to communicate his thoughts to the kid. So, he asked his son to go and ask his friend to come over to their house. At that moment, Martín did not feel like having Mo come to his house and make fun of the lack of things visibly seen in his humble apartment. His dad however, knew how to live with plenty and with little, and was not going to allow his current financial situation to dictate his kid's friendships. He was also trying to inculcate values to his son that were independent from any monetary prejudice. For this reason, he made sure that his son went to this young kid Mo and invited him to the house. The plan was that Mo would call his house to let his parents know that he was safe and not wandering the streets. – But dad, he likes to be outside –, commented Martín. – Son, no one likes to be alone in the dark without a place to go –, replied Victor, while fixating his eyes on his son, as if his message was even more clear than any other time. It certainly was, Martín went to Mo and invited him to his apartment. Although Mo was a bit hesitant to the invitation, at the end he accepted and thanked not only Martín but also Victor and Adriana. It seemed for Mo that this new kid called Martín would become a friend.

Shortly after arriving to his apartment that night, Mo called his dad who ended up passing by to pick up his son. Mo told his dad not to come upstairs but that he would wait for him downstairs by the entrance. He felt ashamed of his dad's appearance, and he was well aware that his dad suffered from alcoholism and that by this time in the evening, he would have had a few drinks already. He did not want his new friend or the dad to know that his own father had an illness, and therefore, after speaking with his dad, he mentioned to Martín that his dad would be waiting for him downstairs. Victor was okay with that but at the same time asked Martín and Adriana to accompany Mo to the front door when it was time for Mo to go downstairs. Both kids did not object and did exactly what their dad had asked for. Soon Mo's dad came and picked up his son. He patted his son on top of the head and greeted to the two siblings. Adriana noticed the alcohol smell coming out of his breath but did not say anything to Martín. However, the moment she arrived home, she made sure to make her own father aware of it. Her brother on the other hand, was beginning to feel a glimpse of contentment from making a new friend. He knew that Mo was no Waldo, and was mindful that maybe he would never become one, but was rather thankful that now he had a friend and not an enemy.

The friendship blossomed and these two continued to hang out together in the park while playing baseball with Martín's dad and at school, also while part-taking in the same sport with the other kids. Nonetheless, as the saying goes "all things must come to an end" and unfortunately for Martín, after becoming fond of Mo, his friend suddenly left the school. Their comradeship ended abruptly for both kids, as Mo was taken away from his dad by child services a few days before the end of school. Martín felt sad once again and felt the loss of yet another friend. This one gave him a tough time for the longest time, but it was something that he remembered with joy and sadness.

Chapter 13 – The Departure of Mo

The situation at Mo's house with his dad continued decaying on a daily basis. It seemed like Mo was taking care of a non-functional parent, who needed help even for the day-to-day small tasks. Mo quickly had to leave his childhood behind and mature, in order to tend for his own needs and those of his dad. He found himself cleaning after Isak and even providing some kind of food that he often took from the snack program at school. He became an expert of putting together a plate of macaroni and cheese, accompanied by apple slices and baby carrots that Isak either picked up at a food stamp location, or that Mo had grabbed from the school's food bank, without anyone noticing. There were times that his classmates would bring a non-perishable item to be donated, and once these items were placed on the table in the back corner of the room, Mo would calculate his every move to snatch a few items and place them in his bag without having anyone notice. However, what he did not know is that his own teacher noticed, and without saying anything to Mo, the teacher decided to put the most necessary items like canned milk, tuna fish, pasta and sauce, including pudding and some sweet dessert, either on the top, or at a desk that had easier access for Mo to grab without leaving behind any trace. The teacher had a feeling that the finances in Mo's house was not the best, and that any help that his dad could use, would be provided for. He noticed this when he realized that Mo sometimes would bring a lunch and oftentimes would come to class hungry. In fact, on one occasion, Mo was doing a reading comprehension activity in front of his teacher, and his stomach orchestrated a symphony of hunger and poor eating morning habits, that quickly triggered his teacher to acknowledge this as part of an unbalanced eating problem. For this reason, his teacher started a "bring a canned good campaign" for donations that were needed in a nearby food bank. Nevertheless, he knew that part of those items would be used by anyone in his class that truly needed them. He did this thinking specifically of Mo and others like him. The student's response was overwhelming, as everyday it seemed that the pile of goods would grow, not allowing anyone to notice that the mountain of food did actually diminish due to the needs of Mo. Except for once when one of the lads who had brought a few things, noticed that those were not there anymore. – Hey… my tuna cans and macaroni and cheese are not here anymore – , he announced with a stern voice, alarming the class to come and corroborate the findings. However, after noticing that Mo's face turned red and was discomforted, the teacher asserted that some of the items were not there because he had already dropped them off at the food bank, to make room for other future ones. His reply came out very automatic and seemed premeditated. Perhaps because his educator's instincts came out as agile as a feline hopping from tree to tree, which allowed for a quick response that was well accepted by everyone, and quickly turning off any signs of fire. It was in that moment that Mo understood that his teacher had allowed him to take certain items, and though he did not voice his gratitude, the smile imprinted on his face, said it all. His teacher did not want to hurt his student's pride and did not mention anything but continued to scavenge the healthier and easier to cook items and kept on placing them on top, for easier access.

  Mo quickly became very good at preparing meals for his dad and for himself. He figured that if this was the way life had to be, then he would try making it the best one possible. He was very thankful for the support his teacher was providing him, even though his teacher had not mentioned it out loud. He was not the only kid that took advantage of this service, but no one in the class, or in the school ever found out who the blessed ones were. It was important for the teacher and for the kids to remain anonymous. Although Mo started to have some positive outcomes, he still could quickly become enraged when he would think of his family.

Mo would often compare his dad with Martín's, and would think that life was not fair. "How could it be that I don't have a mom with me and the only parent I have is one who is a "drunken bum"". He would try not to take his anger against Martín, or let this envy govern his mentality, nonetheless, sometimes it was uncontrollable to do so. This would lead to hurting his new friend, Martín who would go home, upset and quiet, and mope on his own. It was tough for Martín to realize that his new friend only acted aggressively due to what he lacked, which impeded him to have a normal life as a kid. Furthermore, seeing Martín with two loving parents and a big sister, just made him at times react juvenile. Martín disliked him when he was rude and aggressive. This situation made him miss his buddy, Waldo. His parents would try to help him understand that Mo acted in such way due to the lack of love and guidance that he had in his life. – Do you remember how difficult it was to live in Peru without your daddy? – mom asked, at times to a sobbing Martín, who did not need to verbalize an answer in order to be understood by his mom. – Now imagine never meeting your mom at all. How would your life change? Would you be as happy as you are? – These questions did help him put things into perspective, nevertheless, the pain suffered from an oftentimes rude Mo, would not become any less. Martín's mom gave him different coping strategies when dealing with an aggressive kid like Mo, and had her son practice these with her, in order to help him be a friend but not get hurt in the process. She still knew that it was important to be nice to those who don't deserve it, especially if they are hurting inside. This meant that he would take an approach of voicing his feelings right away when Mo mistakenly hurt his buddy, or even to walk away from him and say "I am not playing anymore" which would trigger Mo a need to change his behavior. He also learned at times to ignore the bad conduct. All of these strategies did work as long as Martín was consistent and did not allow himself to become a floor mat. Putting limits on negative and unwanted behaviors were fundamental in reminding Mo that although he was accepted, he could not misuse a friendship.

Regardless of the tough times and the irritating moments that Martín would tell you about his new friendship with Mo, he enjoyed having a buddy around. In addition, their love for the game of baseball was something they had in common that often brought them together. Polishing their skills during what they called "intense practices" during lunch time and even after school, was what definitely showed their commitment to the game. However, the practices did not only mean this for Martín, it also signified a strong bond of a friendship that he longed to have. Things seemed to perk up for a short time for Martín, and besides being together with his dad, he was also starting to show happiness for coming to Canada. This meant that his mind did not travel as much to his home country, as it usually did, especially during class. What kid doesn't daydream during class? One question that even his teachers would often ask was how and why his family did choose to come to Canada. This was not easy to answer, particularly if you do not have the appropriate vocabulary to express your thinking. Nevertheless, it would allow Martín to reminisce about his dad's journey when he came to this beautiful land.

Only having worked for two months and finding favour in the eyes of his boss at the local supermarket, where by now he had worked for two months in New Jersey, Victor was asked to come into the boss's office (the interesting thing was that Victor was known to his boss by a different name, a 'legal' name).

– Rolando, please come in and see Mr. McDonald –, asked the boss's secretary, pointing towards the office. Victor imagined that his time of work at this supermarket in New Jersey had come to an end. He quickly, picked up the remainder of the fruit inside a box and placed it neatly on top of the others, making a pyramid of apples. He then wiped his hands clean with the apron he was wearing, took it off and left it on his cart, and made his way to the office to find out his fate…

– Mr. MacDonald –, pronounced Victor with a very thick Spanish accent.

– Yes! Hi, come in, Rolando. Please have a seat –. At the beginning, Victor was perplexed for even being invited into the office, as the only time he'd been there was when he was hired. The kindness of his boss throughout his time working at the market was not only evident to Victor, but rather to every employee, young and old. However, he did not understand the reason for him being called into the office, except for that the boss may have found out his immigration status; a thought that kept on creeping into his head every day.

– Please, call me Jimmy, *por favor*– added the boss. This made Victor smile, not because he asked him to call him by his first name but because Mr. McDonald had tried speaking Spanish.

– Yes, Mr… Jimmy– continued Victor.

– Listen I know about you. I know you are not Rolando. You have another name. Please tell me what is your name? – inquired the boss. Victor understood quite well what his boss was saying but he did not know how to answer. In the moment that he was about to answer, the office door opened again and it was the secretary letting his boss know that the other guest was present. "Okay, great!" informed Mr. McDonald. "Have him come in, please". A man wearing a slick and formal pin-stripe suit came in, quickly greeting Mr. McDonald and Victor.

– *Mi nombre es abogado Ramirez* –, pronounced the lawyer, introducing himself. Suddenly Victor's eyes opened up to the fullest extent possible, showing off his dark brown iris and kept on thinking, "this is it!" His journey in the United States of America would be over.

– Rolando, if I asked Mr. Ramirez to come here it is because I want to help you. I know that your name is not Rolando. I would like to know what it is. I know that you are in this country illegally, and that you have a family that you send most of your paycheck to. Please let me help you out –, ended Mr. McDonald.

Thank God, that Mr. Ramirez was there to interpret, not necessarily what was said by Mr. McDonald but rather what Victor had to say. In fact, Victor, although at the beginning was shocked to hear what he heard and a bit cynical, opened up and did share his story about his family, going back to the start, from the moment they were all at the embassy line up. Mr. McDonald understood Victor's dilemma and assured him that his lawyer, Mr. Ramirez would work for him, to help him get his legal documents, in addition to getting his family to the United States of America. Victor did not know what to say. He was stunned and could only display gratitude by shaking both men's hands several times. His boss shared with Victor that his dad too came to this country as an immigrant from Scotland, when he was very young. He was dating the lady who later became his wife, the boss's mom, and once he gathered enough money, went back to Scotland, married her and brought her over the Atlantic to settle in the same place they have lived for the last fifty years. In spite of having a successful life in North America, their beginnings were modest and at times lacking many things. However, it was one of their favourite periods throughout the couple's relationship, for they relied on each other. Mr. McDonald was not alive when his parents came to the United States, as a matter of fact, he was born a few years after. However, he knew his parent's financial struggles because his dad made sure to repeat his humble beginning stories every possible time. This is why Mr. McDonald felt compelled to help Victor. Victor tried understanding while listening attentively to what the boss had to say, and thanks to the interpreter, and the lawyer, he was able to express his admiration towards his boss and his parents. The three had a coffee and once finished, Victor, thanked them once again and agreed with the lawyer to meet at a different time to go over his legal case as well as how to go about bringing his family over. He then shook both men's hands and made his way towards the exit, but paused the moment he arrived at the door. He then turned around, faced Mr. McDonald and said to him, *–Me* name is Victor–. Mr. McDonald smiled and said, *–Gracias amigo*, my name is Jimmy, your friend–. As soon as Victor left the office Mr. McDonald continued speaking with his lawyer friend and reminded him that all costs would be relinquished through his office and no bill should be delivered to his employee. Mr.

Ramirez understood his client's desires and assured him that he would also try his best to get Victor's family here.

Time passed and Victor continued to grow as an employee in the business. Mr. McDonald gave him other responsibilities that Victor enjoyed doing. For example, his grocery store offered a delivery service for the elderly, and Mr. McDonald chose Victor to be the person to transport the items to the clients. Victor thought it would be a good way of continuing earning his boss's trust, whereas Mr. McDonald knew that in addition to the wage Victor received from him, the tips that the elderly would reward the delivery man would be plenty to help him save enough money to send to his family. The fact of the matter was that Victor saw favour in all the people he delivered the produce to, given that all of them would give him a juicy tip, at times more than a day's wage. At the beginning, it was difficult for him to accept money from the elderly, since he felt that it was his job to deliver the goods without expecting any other reward other than his own wage. However, all of the clients would not take a 'no' for an answer and extending their arm with the money in hand, they would simply place it in his breast pocket. There was one specific time where a lady who after receiving her bags of produce, asked Victor to step in while she went to get something from the kitchen. Victor complied and waited patiently not knowing what was about to happen. The lady came back with a couple of bills, both twenties, and gave them to him, expecting no refusal, but the moment she saw Victor not accepting the tip, she said to him – this is not for you... this is for your wife and kids. – He did not say anything but a – thank you – shook her hand and was about to step out. At that moment, the lady gave him a big hug and said to him – never forget your family at home. You are a good man and I am glad to be able to help out –, concluded the lady. Victor would count his blessings, though there were too many to keep track of. He was so thankful for the opportunity to work for a philanthropist and be placed in a community full of people who wanted to help him. Quickly he became the client's favourite delivery man.

As promised by Mr. Ramirez, the time came when he and Victor met. They worked arduously with regards to Victor's immigration case. After having enough evidence to build a case, Mr. Ramirez started the paper work. He seemed very optimistic with the process and felt that Victor's family would be able to come to North America. This was Victor's primary question when his family would be able to join him here? Mr. Ramirez would simply encourage him to have patience. He reassured him that time would come when they would be reunited once and forever. This message would give him hope and would fortify his soul. Knowing that his family were that close of coming to North America was fuel to keep on going forward.

The day came when Mr. Ramirez received the first glimpse of hope from immigration, and having shared the good news with his new client, reminded him that step two needed to be developed. This new stage included the reason why Victor was running away from his home country. However, before tackling this part of the process, Victor asked for an estimated time for his family to arrive. The lawyer thought out loud, mumbling a few words and finally expressed,

> – around 4-5 years. Give me that period of time to get them here –, he concluded. Victor could not show any satisfaction for this answer, which threw off the lawyer, given that he was not expecting Victor's reaction.

– No, this is too much time being away from my family. It has almost been eight months since the last time I saw them. I cannot wait that long. My daughter is twelve, she would be a lady the next time I see her? And how about my son? He would be a teenager? This is too long! –, Victor uttered.

– Please, all I ask you is to have some patience and know that I am doing my best to get your family here, as soon as I can. The process takes time. I can promise you three to four years but it might not be feasible. Please allow me to continue working for you and I will do my very best to get them here. –

– *Gracias* –, replied Victor, with sadness stated in his eyes. – I know that you are doing all that is possible and I can only thank you for that. –

Victor shook Mr. Ramirez's hand and thanked him again. He then grabbed his apron and went back to the isle where he was shelving some of the items. – All okay? – asked Mr. McDonald to his employee knowing that there was something bothering him. – Yes, *gracias* –, replied Victor, who extended his hand and once again shook it. This time however, Mr. McDonald felt the sadness transmitted by that handshake. What he did not know but found out the next day, was that Victor decided not to show up for work. In fact, that would be his last day at the supermarket. Victor could not fathom being away from his family for a long period of time, and wanted to be reunited with them. Mr. McDonald could not understand the reason why Victor did not show up, so making his way to Victor's house, he found out that he was not living there anymore. He had left the city, actually he had left...

Victor felt very unsettled knowing that his wife and kids were back at home suffering much economical need on top of political turmoil, social instability and missing him. He too missed them and was willing to give it all he had gained, to see them soon. The moment he was in his room thinking about what would be the fastest way to be reunited with his family, he received a phone call from a relative who already lived in Canada. The call could not have come at a better time. In fact, it came just as he was reflecting on his whole journey and whether it had been worth being away from his family. This relative however, reminded him of the sacrifice he had endured to get to where he was, and suggested to go North. "Canada is the new American Dream! You will be a Canadian before you know it, and your family will be here faster than you can imagine it." After their call, Victor thought of the idea to cross the US-Canada border. He was about six to seven hours away from Canada and thought that if Canada would not accept him, he would only be sent back home. He had nothing to lose but everything to gain. He thought that this new opportunity could lead to having his family in North America quicker. He continued started packing his belongings and asked his nephew to take him to the bus station where he would board a Greyhound which would lead him to Buffalo, New York. He also left two letters behind with his nephew and asked him to deliver these two to the appropriate people. His nephew was sad that his uncle would leave. He did though comply with the letters and delivered them; one to Mr. McDonald, thanking him for everything he had done for him, in addition to explaining his next steps, and the other one to his family back at home.

The goodbye with his nephew was one of the greyest moments that both would tell you about. However, Victor reminded him that soon he would be back, and not alone, but rather with the entire family. Trying to comfort his nephew, Victor, reminded the young man to always be a person who does good to others. He also told him that he would remember him as a caring and loving person. His nephew did not want to let go of his uncle yet ended up doing so with distress, not showing his emotions that governed his green eyes. Victor got out of the vehicle, and looking towards his nephew, he waved back with certainty that they would be back together.

The six-hour ride felt like an eternity, which actually allowed Victor time to think of what to say the moment he faced an immigration officer. Eventually the bus made its final stop, showing Victor his new destination, Canada. The border between Canada and the USA was empty, not a soul around, except for the border officers policing the area. Victor made his way to the gate, carrying a bag full of clothing and hope. Entering the gate, he was suddenly welcomed by a border patrol – *bienvenue au Canada* –, with a warm smile drawn on his face. Victor expressed his gratitude and then was asked for his documents. He pretended to look in his pockets, patting each of them and opening and closing his jacket. He finally said – I no have. I refugee –. –Oh, ok. Sir, please come this way–, retorted the officer, and took him to a vehicle and transported him to what seemed to be a detention centre where there were other officers in the foyer. He then told Victor to follow the assigned officer, who would tell him what would happen next. Victor was full of nervousness but tried his best not to show any anxious emotions. He followed the officer. The next officer had some understanding of Spanish and heard Victor's refugee plea, only interrupting when needed. He listened attentively and filled out a couple of forms. He then took Victor to a big room that had couches, tables, and a refrigerator filled with a few days' worth of food and drinks. There were also other men there and all the men had the same thing in common with Victor; they were all detainees. They had also tried their luck to cross into Canada, to start a new life. Some of them were fathers, others were young adults looking for new dreams. One of them approached Victor and welcomed him to his new temporary home. – Hi *amigo* –, he greeted Victor. – My name is Raúl. Tell me, how did you get here –, inquired the man. Victor mentioned his new plan of coming to Canada and then told Raúl that he was there for a couple of days only and that once the long weekend was over, he would be let go. This is what he was told by the last officer, given that Victor had crossed the border on Canada Day and the immigration office at the border was closed until the next business day. Raúl could not help but laugh and made Victor feel naïve. He then took Victor around the room and introduced several men, pointing out how each one of them had been living in that building for the past two weeks, three months, and even eight months. He also pointed out that all of them were promised freedom quickly after arriving. Nonetheless, the promise had started to become nothing but a memory of the past. Victor then said – no, it is different with me, as I was told to listen for my name being called tomorrow when the officer comes and takes me back to the border –. – Ha, ha, ha –, laughed many of the men residing with Raúl and Victor. – Okay, *amigo*–, mentioned Raul, – make sure you grab a pillow, a blanket and a toothbrush. Make yourself at home and don't forget to sign up for cleaning duty–, finalized Raúl. Victor knew that he could not let the people's uncertainty put him down. He wanted to believe that he would be called the next day.

The following morning came and the rays of the summer days woke Victor earlier than ever. Actually, the fact that he was nervous also allowed him to end his slumber earlier than everyone else. He only had time to brush his teeth, given that soon after this, he was called by the same officer who had dropped him off the evening before – Mr. Victor, please come to the main door –, was the alarm that awoke everyone else, including Raúl. Victor knew that his time to meet a new destiny was a few minutes away. Before he met the officer, he went to Raúl and gave him a few belongings that he had collected at the detention centre, and with a heart full of good sentiment, he told Raúl, – I hope to meet you on the other side –. Raúl smiled and thanked him and also said – I wish you all the best, *amigo* –. Victor then departed and met the officer who ended up taking him to the border where the immigration officer was already waiting for him. A short moment after, arrived a lady with her brother who had heard the night before that there was a fellow Peruvian in need of a guarantor, in order to be freed. The lady and her brother took Victor to a city called Mississauga where Victor then would be established, work and find himself a small apartment where his family would later call home.

Martín gazed out the window and kept on living and reliving this moment. Of course, it was not difficult to do, as his dad was a story teller and would retell the same event again and again. – Wow – would be what Martín often said, showing how mesmerized he felt every time his dad shared the time he crossed into Canada. – Remembering is reliving twice the good moments – was what Victor would often tell his kids. That of course, if the memories were worthy of recalling. He was very thankful for the opportunity of coming to Canada, especially after undergoing several struggles that in the end were used for good. As for Mo... His life took a 180 degree turn because the situation with his dad came to a premature end. Children's Aid became involved, after receiving an anonymous call from a neighbour, explaining the sad situation for the boy. Against his will, Mo had to be taken away from his dad and placed under the care of a family that would tend to all of his needs. This meant that Mo's life would become stable with regards to having a place to stay and would have all of his main needs met. Sooner than expected he was adopted by the same family. The interesting thing was that the foster father happened to know Isak very well: it was Chris who had met Isak and had helped him with coming to Canada. Chris did not want to 'steal Isak's son or take him away from his dad, but understood that Mo needed a stable home and Isak needed help. Chris was willing to support both of them but could only help the child, by opening his house to him. He also desired to help his friend Isak, but the latter's pride and lack of agreement, made it difficult if not impossible to get the appropriate support. With time though, both men were able to have had a heart-to-heart conversation. With Isak's blessings and promise to finally get help, Mo moved in with his new family but unfortunately for him and for his new friend, Martín, he had to leave his neighbourhood, including his school.

Chapter 14 – Terror with a Sweet Victory

–Yes... yes... officer. I understand the situation. I will make sure I get home as soon as possible... thank you for your concerns and for your support–, ended Victor. It was a conversation that turned his world upside down. It had been a few years since Victor lived the vengeance and terror out of the hands of a revolutionary movement that trumped over anyone standing in the way of its ideals. The last time Victor had any dealings with this pseudo-political group, he ended up on a bed in the intensive care unit at the hospital. Now, after several years of peace and flying under the radar, the same group was back again and it was the same one who orchestrated the death of Victor's uncle. Having the same name of his uncle, Victor knew that this group was not going to stop until their bullets reached him and his family. "What am I to do?" Was one of his queries he often stumbled upon. This was one of the main motivations to leave his country and try his luck elsewhere, hoping that he could once and for all, escape the destructive hands of a power-hungry group. The situation had gone from bad to worse, and all in a matter of a few years. As for his family, they had suffered tremendous loss, not only monetarily but rather, the loss of lives of loved ones, like his uncle, and later his cousin too. Victor was not willing to risk his life or that of his own kids and wife. This was the main reason why he left his beautiful homeland, with the hope of bringing his family to wherever he would land.

Canada offered Victor a lawyer, who took care of many of the legal papers he needed to put in place, such as, a working permit, a health card and a refugee claim. Soon he met with this lawyer the same way he had done so with Mr. Ramirez in New Jersey. The process seemed the same, however, one specific detail was different; this lawyer wanted to get the family to immigrate to Canada as soon as possible. He understood the urgency of the matter, not only to keep a family together but also because the evidence pointed towards a direct target… the family. This made the lawyer push for a faster hearing, and preparing for one, he asked his client, Victor, to work on his case, sharing specific events from the horrific times he endured. Victor agreed. He knew that if reminiscing and recalling these events could give him a chance to stay permanently in Canada, in addition to bringing over his family, then it was worth the sacrifice.

    The day of trial came faster than expected. Victor and his lawyer were meeting outside of an immigration office where both of them would have to present Victor's case to the judge and his team. Victor's stomach could not feel any more insecure since the lack of food made loud gastrointestinal noises. The hunger however, made Victor feel more alert and subsequently, be able to share his story with the group in the courtroom. His time came, and both he and his lawyer were invited in. Right away Victor noticed the pale emotionless faces that surrounded the room, decorating it with gloomy, yet professional, and dull feelings that made anyone feel the rattling of his own bones. His lawyer introduced his client and made way for Victor to start his discourse. Good thing for Victor that the judge and the legal team all spoke Spanish and were able to comprehend more than just the gist of the dissertation. Victor started his case with what had just happened to his uncle one year ago. He then linked both his uncle and his own name in putting him at risk, and continued to express to those in the courtroom about the two 'almost tragic' and life threating scenarios when working at the bank. He explained his role as a chartered accountant and what his line of occupation entailed. He clearly explained that as a professional, he had to do what was right and not what was convenient for him. He knew that he had to fight professional accounting related crimes, even if this meant to become "the enemy" of the terrorist group known as *Sendero Luminoso* (or in English as "The Shining Path"). What he did not know was that this would lead him to exactly that, the enemy of the terrorist group that was starting to flourish, which meant that you were either with them or against them. Victor was forced to take a stance, and he did, though not thinking too much of the consequences that led him to be hospitalized twice. He did not leave his country and was not thinking of doing so, however, the moment he found out that one of his relatives who happened to have the same name as him was murdered, then he knew in his heart that it was time to flee. "They were coming for me", he surmised, while extending his hand with copies of a popular Peruvian magazine covering the story of the death of his uncle, in addition to the two life attempts against himself. He continued showing the evidence and the reasons why his family was the next target, and why he had the need for a refugee claim, for himself and for his family.

Twenty minutes, which was the time that took Victor to show his case, could not had passed faster than now. His lawyer signalled Victor to end his discourse twice, given that the first time, did not work. This second time indeed did work, and by the time Victor collected his notes and evidence, he looked up to the judge and the team, to find out that all of them had one thing in common, tears. Victor was asked to step out of the courtroom for what seemed to be the longest five minutes of his life. Without his lawyer or a companion, he sat down inside a white pod with no windows and with one fluorescent tube illuminating the room. Then entered his lawyer... in a very unprofessional manner, as he could not contain his happiness. He was howling happily, uttering "YOU WILL STAY! Your family will come as soon as possible, you will stay, *amigo*". Good thing that his lawyer also spoke some Spanish and was able to convey the message using this same language, although it was probably not needed, given that his emotions and demeanor said it all. He hugged his client and even kissed his cheek saying – there is not one person in that courtroom who does not want your family to be here! – Victor, shocked with the news, could not allow his face and body to drain his emotions. He was simply in shock, but in a good way, if you can say that. He could only think of thanking his lawyer and even wanted to go back in the courtroom to shake everyone's hand in there. However, the officer by the door would not allow anyone in the courtroom without first having the permission from the judge. Regardless of the case, Victor thanked the officer by the door, and mentioned to him to please extend his gratitude towards the others on his behalf. The officer smiled and shook his hand and also promised that he would do exactly that. Whether he did or did not, did not matter for Victor, as the emotions that he was starting to experience felt like the burst of a bottle of champagne ready for a celebration.

    Victor did not know how to thank his lawyer more than shaking his hand and mentioning over and over – thank you, thank you thank you, sir –. After signing a few more forms and his lawyer explaining the next steps to an absentminded Victor, as he was still in shock, he decided to end the meeting soon, with a fast approaching meeting to go over the same details from that day. He drove Victor to his dwelling and congratulated him once again. After saying goodbye and waiting for his lawyer to drive away Victor entered the house where he lived, then, in his own room and seeing his own bed, he dropped by the foot of it and sobbed, letting all of his emotions pour out still not believing the favourable outcome... If you had seen him in this situation, you would have expected the worst news possible, and this is what the owner of the house, the lady who picked him up from the border, thought. She did not understand the pain that he was feeling, yet she let him be, not knocking on the door to his room to interrupt him. Several minutes passed, and Victor got up from the ground, wiped up his tears, went to his window and saw the deep blue sky and uttered a "thank you". He then got out of his room to go to the kitchen and prepare himself a coffee. This is where he noticed that the owner of the house was home. She had already prepared the java, and having placed two cups, one for her and one for him, he sat down. – My family is coming –, he pronounced with a deep red face and glossy eyes that still reflected a waterfall more than anything else. There were no other words that were pronounced. Victor showed his refugee claim document with the green stamp to her, and without hesitations received a hug from the lady. – You and your family will be united before you know it. I am so glad for you and them. – – Thank you –, replied Victor but not only for her best wishes but rather for everything that she represented. In fact, she was the means that let him to be allowed into the country.

Victor loved sharing this story with his family. The first time was over the phone, but now with them by his side, he could not stop himself from retelling it over and over. His family did not seem to mind. In fact, his kids would always ask their daddy to remind them of his experiences from the moment he left Peru. He did not mind reliving these anecdotes and sharing them with the people he loved the most. A parent's love cannot be measured, however, it seems like that love becomes exponential the moment you add distance and time being apart from each other to the equation. These were the moments he anticipated having, seated on a couch with his wife and having his son on his lap and his daughter leaning on him. The scenario, although different, given that it was now in a smaller apartment, still meant a world to the now united family. Though their new dwelling was humble and lacked several pieces of furniture, it felt full with everyone back together again.

Chapter 15 – The Surprise

Close to a year had passed and I missed my friend Mo, and was never able to play baseball with him again. He and I had gone through good and bad times. Many fights (mainly because of him) brought us together. It is interesting that my parents were able to have compassion towards the boy who irritated me day after day. They did not see a bully, but rather a kid in need; a lost soul searching for acceptance and belonging; a child longing for a family, as much as my parents, my sister and I longed to be together. My mom focused on the bigger picture. It took me time to do the same, but with their support, I was also able to take off the veil of hatred and resentment that impeded me from seeing his suffering. I missed Mo. The class missed him too. Even our teacher missed him, especially when noticing that the pile of donated food was not diminishing like before. Everyone wished him the best.

One day the unexpected happened. We were in class when the office buzzed our teacher, asking permission to have someone come to the office and pick up some flyers. The teacher chose me to go. I did not refute, but rather stopped my work, placed my pencil on my desk and went down the hallway towards the office. In that small space, there seemed to be a parent with a child speaking with the secretary and the principal. I continued to walk. I was not sure what to expect but when I saw what I saw, my heart jumped out of my chest, skipping a beat when I saw the face of my friend Mo. He was there, happy and he looked older and cleaner, in fact, well taken care of. The man who brought him over was his foster dad, who should receive all of the credit for Mo's change. However, at that point I don't think anyone in the class, including me, thought very highly of this man. It took my mom a lot of explaining to help me understand that this man gave Mo and his dad a second chance. An opportunity to change. Mo ran to me and gave me a hug. He was happier to see me than I could ever have imagined. He asked about my family, like it was his own. I told him that my parents still kept him in their prayers, wishing him all the best. He asked his foster dad and the office if it was okay for us two kids to go back to the class to say hi to everyone else. The principal thought it was a fantastic idea. Chris, the foster father, also agreed. Both of us decided to catch up quickly and talk about the baseball team and our own training. We also hoped of playing in the same team. Mo had moved to an affluent area, whereas my family continued to live in the same neighbourhood that had opened its doors first to my dad and then to us all. Although Mo did not suffer any need, he did not forget his humble beginnings, and the times that he "borrowed" items from his class to feed himself and his dad. He also did not forget the times he ate a humble yet nutritious meal at my house. He was so thankful for all of this. The catching up ended the moment both of us neared the classroom and one of the peers announced to the class that Mo was back. Though a school year had passed and of course we were all one year older, our class remained the same, with the same teacher. Everyone without even thinking to ask the teacher for permission, made their way towards the door and chanting his name, they all gave him a big squeeze. The teacher was so glad to have seen him. He invited him into the classroom and asked everyone to make a circle on the carpet, and having Mo sit between me and the teacher, he asked him to update everyone about his new school and new home. Mo was so pleased to see everyone and although he had a lot to share, he rather listened to what had happened in his school while he was gone.

Chris and the principal approached the classroom and saw all of the kids seated on the carpet, sharing stories and exchanging a few laughs. The sense of happiness filled the room and made both the principal and Chris happy. There was a moment where Chris felt sorry for taking Mo out of his homeschool and though he did not share his thoughts aloud, the principal understood the sadness in his eyes and thanked Chris for making a child have an opportunity to succeed, and most importantly, a family.

The time came when Mo had to leave his former peers, and saying goodbye to each one of them, he reminded them that he would not forget them. He then came to me, his buddy, and gave me what seemed to be a gift that Chris was holding. It was inside a plastic bag. He instructed me not to open it until I got home. I took the gift and agreed on the conditions, and then expressed my gratitude. Mo interjected and mentioned that he needed to be the one to show gratitude, not only to me but to my entire family. He was so thankful that my family became the type that sought for his needs without any prejudice. He did not know how to ever thank us and hoped that the small gift could somehow be liked by everyone. I extended my arm as a gesture to shake his hand, however, Mo pulling me towards him, gave me a great hug. He also apologized for all of his wrongdoings against me, reminding me of all of the name callings and putdowns I had endured due to his negative actions. I then grabbed Mo by the neck and said, – it's okay! –. We both hugged it out one last time and then Mo followed his foster father to the exit. I was so happy to have seen my friend but at the same time I felt sad to see yet another friend leave my life.

Soon after Mo left the school, it was time for dismissal. The peers were all still talking about Mo, and were expressing their gladness for having seen him once again. Even though I felt happy for having also been with him, I was sad and felt like not talking about it. I prepared my backpack and made my way home, holding the bag that Mo and Chris, his foster father, had given me.

When I got home I could not wait to tell my family of Mo's visit to the school, but having an empty apartment, for at least five minutes until Adriana arrived from her school, I opened the bag, to find two gifts. One was two brand new baseball gloves, one for me and the other one for my dad, and a card with some cash that Chris wanted to share with my family. He knew that our financial situation as a new immigrant family was a struggle and wanted to bless us with this small token. He also knew that my parents would use this money to purchase groceries. In fact, that is precisely what my parents used the money for... four months' worth of food!

I would never hear from Mo again, as his new home with Chris and his wife and kids was far from where I lived. However, the excitement of having seen my friend and knowing that he was in better hands, filled my heart with joy instead of aches. I mean, what is more important in life is to have a loving family with you, always. Amidst our economic change, we felt like the richest family of all. We were together! We were safe! We enjoyed so much as a family and overcame several obstacles on the way. We felt God's presence in our lives and we became eternally grateful to Him, who made and continues to make in all things good for those who love Him.

Years passed by and there is so much I can say about my sister and me, and of course, our parents. We could talk about more hardships we encountered, including missing our extended family back in Peru. However, what I will say is that in Canada we were offered a safe home, a valuable education, and an opportunity to enjoy the numerous cultures and foods our new home had to offer. Here we learned to not take anything for granted; we found the love of the Almighty and felt his immeasurable grace and providence; we felt safe and had the opportunities to grow and become a blessing to others in the jobs we do. When we left our beloved Peru, we did so because we could not stay there any longer. Just like any immigrant in this country, we lived with half of our heart, as the other part stayed back in our place of birth, with our extended family and friends, until our hearts were won by Canada, and slowly but surely, we became Canadians!

– The End –

Made in the USA
Monee, IL
15 November 2020